Countering the Risks of North Korean Nuclear Weapons

BRUCE W. BENNETT, KANG CHOI, MYONG-HYUN GO,
BRUCE E. BECHTOL, JR., JIYOUNG PARK, BRUCE KLINGNER,
DU-HYEOGN CHA

RAND NATIONAL SECURITY RESEARCH DIVISION

THE ASAN INSTITUTE
for POLICY STUDIES

For more information on this publication, visit www.rand.org/t/PEA1015-1

Library of Congress Cataloging-in-Publication Data is available for this publication.
ISBN: 978-1-9774-0676-7

Published by the RAND Corporation, Santa Monica, Calif.
© Copyright 2021 RAND Corporation
RAND® is a registered trademark.

Cover image: Korean Central News Agency

Support RAND
Make a tax-deductible charitable contribution at
www.rand.org/giving/contribute

www.rand.org

About This Perspective

This Perspective describes a combined research effort from the RAND Corporation and the Asan Institute for Policy Studies focused on the North Korean nuclear weapon threat. Drawing on open sources, we describe the current and developing nature of the threat posed by North Korean nuclear weapons and then propose actions that the Republic of Korea (ROK) and the United States could take to counter that threat.

This project has been a team effort by the authors identified on the title page. We appreciate the funding from the Asan Institute for Policy Studies and the interest of the Asan founder and honorary chairman, M. J. Chung.

We also appreciate the formal substantive reviews performed by Jim Quinlivan of RAND, COL (Ret.) David Maxwell of the Foundation for Defense of Democracies, and Soo Kim of RAND. We also appreciate comments from Choi Jinwook (Korea Institute for National Unification), GEN (Ret.) Jang Hyok (ROK Army), Kim Sung-han (Korea University), Kim Yong-ho (Korea National Defense University), Park Changkwon (Korea Institute for Defense Analyses), Sheen Seong-ho (Seoul National University), GEN (Ret.) Ryu Jae-seung (ROK Army), GEN (Ret.) Lee Jong-sup (ROK Army), Syd Seiler (National Intelligence Council), Brad Roberts (Lawrence Livermore National Laboratory), Lee Hyun-seung (North Korean escapee), and MAJ Garrett Close (U.S. Army).

This research was sponsored by the Asan Institute for Policy Studies and conducted within the International Security and Defense Policy Center of the RAND National Security Research Division (NSRD). NSRD conducts research and analysis for the Office of the Secretary of Defense, the U.S. Intelligence Community, the U.S. State Department, allied foreign governments, and foundations.

For more information on the RAND International Security and Defense Policy Center, see www.rand.org/nsrd/isdp or contact the director (contact information is provided on the webpage).

Contents

Figures and Tables

Figures

Tables

Summary

Since failing to conquer and control the Republic of Korea (ROK) in the 1950–1953 Korean War, the leaders of North Korea have sought dominance of the Korean Peninsula. However, they have lacked the economic, political, and conventional military means to achieve that dominance. Instead, their nuclear weapon and ballistic missile programs have become their means for empowering their regime and working toward dominance. Today, even a few of the likely dozens of North Korean nuclear weapons could cause millions of fatalities and serious casualties if detonated on ROK or U.S. cities.[1] Unfortunately, the major ROK and U.S. strategy to moderate the growing North Korean nuclear weapon threat has been negotiating with North Korea to achieve denuclearization, and this effort has failed and seems likely to continue failing.[2] Despite some ROK and U.S. efforts to enhance defense and deterrence, there is a growing gap between the North Korean nuclear weapon threat and ROK and U.S. capabilities to defeat it. Because these capabilities will take years to develop, the ROK and the United States must turn their attention to where the threat could be in the mid to late 2020s and identify strategy options that can be employed in the coming years to counter it. To simplify doing so, we estimate (in Chapter Three of this Perspective) that, by 2027, North Korea could have 200 nuclear weapons and several dozen intercontinental ballistic missiles (ICBMs) and hundreds of theater missiles for delivering the nuclear weapons. The ROK and the United States are not prepared, and do not plan to be prepared, to deal with the coercive and warfighting leverage that these weapons would give North Korea.

This Perspective focuses on what the ROK and the United States could do in the coming years to counter the developing North Korean nuclear weapon threat. To

---

[1] For the sake of brevity, most footnote citations are not provided in the Summary, but rather in the main text where each issue is discussed.

[2] There is a rich literature (see Chapter One) arguing that negotiation with North Korea, including more ROK and U.S. compromises, should achieve at least some degree of North Korean denuclearization to keep the North's nuclear weapon threat within a moderate range of a few dozen nuclear weapons. However, according to the National Intelligence Officer for North Korea, Sydney Seiler, "Every engagement in [North Korean] diplomacy has been designed to further the nuclear program, not to find a way out of the nuclear program" (David Volodzko, "North Korea Dangerous But Not Unpredictable, Says US Intelligence Official," NK News, January 22, 2021).

explain the threat that the ROK and the United States must be prepared to counter, we address North Korea's objectives, its nuclear weapon buildup, and how North Korea might use its nuclear weapons once it has developed a nuclear weapon force capable of enabling peninsula dominance. We expect that North Korea will prefer to use its nuclear weapons for coercion and deterrence because such a strategy, supported by 200 nuclear weapons, might be effective in achieving North Korean objectives and might pose less risk to the North Korean regime than nuclear weapon attacks. But the North Korean regime faces internal instabilities and is determined and ruthless; we cannot rule out North Korea trying to manage its internal problems by waging a limited or major diversionary war in which it would use nuclear weapons.

North Korean leader Kim Jong-un appears to be building a nuclear weapon force capable of enabling peninsula dominance. The nuclear weapon threat that North Korea already poses to the ROK—perhaps 50 or more nuclear weapons—is dangerous and requires enhanced ROK and U.S. defenses to sustain deterrence now, as well as efforts designed to build toward even more-capable defenses for countering the 2027 nuclear weapon threat that our analysis anticipates. The ROK and the United States should do so while not abandoning the potential of denuclearization and testing it by challenging Kim to demonstrate some reduction in his nuclear weapon threat.

North Korea's Objectives and the Potential Roles of Its Nuclear Weapons

Since the end of the Korean War in 1953, North Korea has transitioned to a limited war, or cold war, strategy, keeping the country on a partial wartime status and employing heavy indoctrination internally against the North's "enemies": the ROK and the United States. The North has pursued nuclear weapons, recognizing that they offer the potential to empower a weak and impoverished country that is unable to compete economically or with conventional military forces against the ROK and the United States. The North has now tested six nuclear weapons; produced dozens of nuclear weapons while apparently seeking several hundred; and produced hundreds of ballistic missiles, in part for nuclear weapon delivery. The North is a revisionist regional country seeking to redress decades of Japanese occupation and U.S. domination, in part by being recognized as a nuclear weapon state and a peer of the United States. Obtaining such recognition would make the regime appear to be a success, demonstrating its ability to overcome its own "century of humiliation" and return to regional-power status, a status experienced by some of the historical Korean dynasties, such as Koguryeo. Meanwhile, Kim Jong-un is fearful of a free and affluent ROK posing an alternative example to the North Korean people.

Within this context, the North Korean regime appears to have three principal objectives:

1. ensure regime survival and maintain absolute control over North Korea
2. achieve peninsula dominance—i.e., Korean unification of some form under regime control
3. make North Korea a regional great power that is able to achieve the first two objectives and to thwart even domination by the United States and China.

Before his death, Kim Jong-il prepared final instructions for his son, telling him that "Unification of two Koreas is the ultimate goal of our family."[3] Unification might allow the Kims to erase many aspects of the dangerous ROK example. But Kim Jong-un also fears the toxic information flow that is already coming into the North; this information flow would only be exacerbated by full unification. Therefore, Kim likely will seek a confederation of some form that would allow him to dominate the peninsula but retain a barrier to outside information reaching his core constituency in the North.

The regime's three objectives are closely interlinked. The regime must survive to accomplish unification and become a great power. According to North Korean escapee Thae Yong-ho, the principal threat to North Korean regime survival is from inside North Korea, because of the failures and brutality of the North Korean regime. But if the regime were to impose a form of Korean unification under its control, the regime likely would hope to be celebrated internally for such a great victory, securing regime survival for some time against internal threats. And by becoming a regional great power, North Korea would be able to dominate the ROK and would hope to break the pattern of U.S. and Chinese dominance of North Korea. If achieved, this outcome would secure regime survival against such outside influences.

From a North Korean perspective, North Korea's nuclear weapons are key to accomplishing these objectives. Although North Korean conventional military forces are numerically superior to ROK and U.S. conventional forces deployed in the ROK, they are qualitatively inferior to the ROK and U.S. forces and thus risk regime survival in a war.[4] The 2013 North Korean Law on Consolidating the Position of Nuclear Weapons State characterizes the nuclear arsenal's role as "deterring and repelling the aggression and attack of the enemy" and as a means to strike "deadly retaliatory blows at the strongholds of aggression until the world is denuclearized."[5] Despite the seven-

---

[3] Jeong Yong-soo, "Kim Jong-il's Final Orders: Build More Weapons," *JoongAng Daily*, January 29, 2013.

[4] Kim Jong-un visited and inspected his forces at the beginning of his reign in 2012 and reached this conclusion in March 2012, according to a presentation by ROK National Assemblyman Thae Yong-Ho to the Institute for Corean-American Studies on December 17, 2020.

[5] "2013 Plenary Meeting of WPK Central Committee and 7th Session of Supreme People's Assembly," North Korean Economy Watch, April 1, 2013.

decade-old U.S. commitment to the ROK, which has been reinforced by every U.S. President, Kim apparently believes that, "if North Korea creates more than 20,000 American casualties in the region, the U.S. will roll back and the North Korea will win the war."[6] Kim's pursuit of a large ICBM force, capable of killing hundreds of thousands to millions of Americans inside the United States, suggests an intent to threaten use of its nuclear weapons as leverage over the United States. A large North Korean nuclear weapon force also might allow the North to resist Chinese efforts at dominance as China attempts to become a global hegemon by 2049 and to exercise influence even beyond the peninsula. Therefore, it should be no surprise that the North Korean regime consistently speaks of its nuclear weapons as a "treasured sword."

North Korea has many ways in which it could use its nuclear weapons as their numbers increase. The North has already been using them for intimidation, coercion, and deterrence. Kim might hope to use the substantial ICBM capability he is preparing in an effort to break U.S. extended deterrence, preventing the United States from retaliating against limited nuclear attacks on U.S. forces. By doing so, he might even break the U.S. alliance with the ROK. In addition, Kim's promise to his people that nuclear weapons would improve the North's economic situation suggests that Kim believes that a large ICBM force could be used to coerce the United States into terminating sanctions against the North and providing other economic benefits. The North could also attempt to sell or otherwise proliferate nuclear weapons. And if the North Korean regime feels desperation with internal instability, it could use its nuclear weapons for limited nuclear attacks or major warfare against the ROK and the United States. In 2012, as a hedge against the ROK resisting North Korean coercion, Kim reportedly ordered the preparation of a war plan for conquering the ROK in seven days. The plan called for the use of major nuclear weapon attacks on key ROK infrastructure starting at the beginning of the attack, with the goal of erasing the ROK and U.S. advantages of qualitative conventional military superiority and the ability of the United States to promptly deploy military forces to the ROK.[7]

ROK and U.S. Options for Countering a 2027 North Korean Nuclear Weapon Threat

In recent years, the United States has focused its deterrence of North Korean use of nuclear weapons on threatening that the North Korean regime will not survive

---

[6]   "North Korean Missile Proliferation," hearing before the U.S. Senate Committee on Governmental Affairs Subcommittee on International Security, Proliferation, and Federal Services October 21, 1997, Washington, D.C.: U.S. Government Printing Office, 1997, p. 5.

[7]   Chung Kyung-young, "Realities and Strategies in Managing North Korea's Nuclear Challenge," *China Quarterly of International Strategic Studies*, Vol. 2, No. 4, 2016, pp. 465–484; and Jeong Yong-soo and Ser Myo-ja, "Kim Jong-un Ordered a Plan for a 7-Day Asymmetric War: Officials," *JoongAng Daily*, January 7, 2015.

nuclear weapon use.[8] The United States has also sought, unsuccessfully, to denuclearize North Korea to prevent its nuclear weapon use, and it now appears clear that Kim will not give up his nuclear weapons. Although North Korea has been deterred from using nuclear weapons in limited or major attacks, some North Korean coercion with nuclear weapons and, reportedly, some North Korean nuclear proliferation have not been deterred. It is also unclear whether the U.S. deterrence threat would work if the regime felt serious internal threats and sought a diversionary war against the ROK and the United States. ROK and U.S. deterrence also might fail if North Korea threatened nuclear attacks against the U.S. homeland to prevent U.S. nuclear retaliation against the regime.

Therefore, looking ahead to the more serious nuclear weapon threat that North Korea might pose by 2027, the ROK and the United States are most likely to deter North Korean nuclear weapon use if they develop the capabilities both to better defend themselves against North Korean nuclear weapon use and to be able to defeat North Korea in whatever way it uses nuclear weapons. The ROK and the United States need to strengthen the ROK-U.S. alliance, orient their plans and procurements to countering the range of possible North Korean nuclear weapon uses, and clearly demonstrate their intent and capability to destroy the regime if it uses nuclear weapons. If the ROK and the United States do so, the North hopefully will conclude that its nuclear weapons are a liability and will be willing to negotiate at least some degree of denuclearization.

Unfortunately, developing ROK and U.S. capabilities that are adequate to defeat North Korean nuclear weapon attacks will take years and likely greater investments than the ROK and the United States are willing to make. Still, the ROK and the United States need to seek capabilities to defeat North Korean nuclear weapon attacks or risk giving North Korea serious leverage against them. And the ROK and the United States should continue to be clear that they do not want a war with North Korea, whether a hot war or a cold war, but are prepared to fight and win if the North pursues war. As the North Korean threat grows, so must ROK and U.S. counters if deterrence and regional stability are to be sustained, especially against a regime that might use nuclear weapons in response to desperate internal circumstances.

The ROK and the United States have a wide variety of options that they can pursue to counter North Korean nuclear weapon use. They must consider putting all options on the table to maximize the effectiveness of their efforts. Some of these options are relatively low-cost. For example, it would cost the U.S. government relatively little to clarify that it is prepared to eliminate the regime if the regime executes major nuclear weapon attacks. It would also cost relatively little to formulate and promulgate U.S. strategy for responding to limited North Korean nuclear weapon attacks. For example, the United States should privately communicate to the North Korean regime that even a single nuclear warhead used to attack Camp Humphreys or other

8   U.S. Department of Defense, *Nuclear Posture Review*, Washington, D.C., February 2018b, p. 33.

major U.S. military bases in Northeast Asia would lead to regime elimination, not U.S. withdrawal from the ROK. Efforts to defend and protect the ROK and U.S. societies and military forces would be more expensive but probably cost-efficient in strengthening deterrence. Obvious choices include enhanced and more-numerous missile defenses, more-dispersed military bases (especially air bases) to deny the North an ideal target set for its nuclear weapons, the ability to promptly disperse ROK and U.S. forces from fixed facilities on warning, and protections against nuclear weapon effects. Also more expensive would be options for enhancing the effects of ROK and U.S. offensive operations against North Korean nuclear weapons and missiles, including high-quality intelligence collection on the North's nuclear forces and leadership, a substantial stand-off capability to destroy both, and an ability to do so preemptively if the North's nuclear weapon threat grows too large. Still, some of these options might be relatively cost-efficient.

The ROK and the United States also could use threats to pressure North Korea. For example, the United States could warn the North that if it appears to have fielded an unacceptable number of nuclear weapons (maybe 80 to 100), the ROK and U.S. might be forced to prepare to execute preemptive counterforce or decapitation attacks, or both. The United States could also threaten North Korea that if it crosses an ICBM or nuclear weapon inventory threshold, or both, the United States will station in the ROK eight to ten tactical nuclear weapons capable of destroying deep underground facilities (where Kim would likely hide after using a nuclear weapon), along with the dual-capable U.S. aircraft required to deliver these weapons. If the number of North Korean ICBMs grows too large, the ROK might question the viability of the U.S. nuclear umbrella and require an ROK nuclear weapon force; the United States should regularly explain this possibility to North Korea and China—a possibility that neither country would want—in the hopes of moderating North Korean nuclear weapon force size.

There is a risk that taking such strong ROK and U.S. actions will sustain or even enhance North Korean hostility. If this happens, North Korea would be more inclined to quicken the pace of its nuclear weapon program and commit more provocations. But the North appears to be expending enormous resources on its nuclear weapon program already and likely cannot do much beyond ongoing efforts to increase its pace.

Therefore, it is critical that the ROK and the United States enhance their efforts to deter North Korean provocations, information operations, and other hostility short of open conflict. In most cases, such efforts require creativity but not major expenditures. For example, the North Korean regime is hypersensitive about outside information and especially outside criticism. The normal ROK and U.S. failure to exploit this sensitivity is no longer acceptable; a major ROK and U.S. information-operations campaign against North Korea should improve deterrence of North Korean actions, from provocations to nuclear weapon attacks. ROK and U.S. information operations could focus on North Korean human rights violations, the corruption of the North Korean government, the opulence of the regime's lifestyle, and the failures of the North Korean regime. The ROK and the United States also need to develop plans to counter a variety of North Korean provocations and limited attacks, determining how to proportionately respond. For example, if North Korea does a ballistic missile test, the ROK and the United States could interdict and seize North Korean ships involved in ship-to-ship transfers to export such cargoes as coal and import such cargoes as oil.

The ROK and the United States should remain open to the possibility of sincere negotiations to reduce the magnitude of the North Korean threat. Even a modest threat reduction would be helpful. If North Korea becomes convinced that the ROK and the United States can and will defeat its nuclear weapon aggression, the North might be willing to negotiate limits on its nuclear weapon program, thereby restoring a greater degree of stability to the region. Unfortunately, North Korea is unlikely to seriously consider any form of denuclearization until it becomes convinced that its nuclear weapons are more of a liability than an asset. And the ROK and the United States must increase their capabilities to defeat North Korean nuclear weapon use if they want to achieve this outcome.

One challenge for the ROK and the United States will be likely Chinese opposition to ROK and U.S. actions to defeat the North Korean nuclear weapon threat. The ROK and the United States need to significantly increase their information operations to convince China that it, too, faces major North Korean nuclear weapon threats, including from North Korean nuclear weapon proliferation. The ROK and the United States should plan to explain their counter–nuclear weapon efforts to China and to offer China options for helping reduce this threat. China's support can be expected only when Chinese leaders perceive a serious threat to their country from North Korea's nuclear weapon developments.

Abbreviations

CFC	Combined Forces Command
CVID	complete, verifiable, and irreversible dismantlement
DPRK	Democratic People's Republic of Korea (North Korea)
HEU	highly enriched uranium
IAEA	International Atomic Energy Agency
ICBM	intercontinental ballistic missile
KT	kiloton
MIRV	multiple independent reentry vehicle
MWE	megawatt-electric
NATO	North Atlantic Treaty Organization
NLL	Northern Limit Line
NPT	Nonproliferation Treaty
OPCON	operational control
ROK	Republic of Korea (South Korea)
TEL	transporter-erector-launcher
THAAD	Terminal High-Altitude Area Defense
UN	United Nations
UNC	United Nations Command
WMD	weapons of mass destruction

CHAPTER ONE

Introduction

There is a substantial literature on the North Korean nuclear weapon threat and options for dealing with it.[1] Much of this literature assumes that North Korea has developed nuclear weapons primarily to deter U.S. attacks against the North, as it has claimed. Many of the experts estimate that North Korea has developed 20 to 60 nuclear weapons to achieve this deterrence and that the North is only slowly increasing these numbers.[2] North Korea has insisted that it was prepared to abandon its nuclear weapon program if the United States ended its hostility toward North Korea.[3] Therefore, much of the literature recommends significant U.S. compromises, such as the signing of a peace treaty or an end-of-war agreement with North Korea, as a precursor to North Korea beginning denuclearization. In addition, despite the fact that North Korea has yet to show good faith by eliminating even a single nuclear weapon, much of the literature expresses hope that the North Korean nuclear weapon threat can be resolved through negotiations with North Korea. Therefore, the ROK and U.S. military forces have taken relatively little action to protect the ROK from North Korean

---

[1]   See, for example, Robert Carlin and Robert Jervis, *Nuclear North Korea: How Will It Behave?* Washington, D.C.: US-Korea Institute at SAIS, October 2015; Stephan Haggard and Tai Ming Cheung, *North Korea's Nuclear and Missile Programs*, San Diego, Calif.: UC Institute on Global Conflict and Cooperation, IGCC Policy Brief, July 2020; Siegfried S. Hecker and Robert L. Carlin, "We Are Teetering on the Edge of a Hinge Point with North Korea," Berggruen Institute, August 5, 2019; Adam Mount, *Conventional Deterrence of North Korea*, Washington, D.C.: Federation of American Scientists, 2019; Mike Mullen, Sam Nunn, and Adam Mount, *A Sharper Choice on North Korea: Engaging China for a Stable Northeast Asia*, New York: Council on Foreign Relations, Independent Task Force Report No. 74, 2016; and Shane Smith, *Implications for US Extended Deterrence and Assurance in East Asia*, Washington, D.C.: US-Korea Institute at SAIS, November 2015b.

[2]   For example, the Stockholm International Peace Research Institute's 2019 yearbook said that North Korea had 20 to 30 nuclear weapons in 2019 and would have 30 to 40 in 2020 (Stockholm International Peace Research Institute, *SIPRI Yearbook 2019: Armaments, Disarmament and International Security*, Oxford, United Kingdom: Oxford University Press, 2019). According to another source, "The size of the country's nuclear stockpile is currently unknown. Pyongyang could have between twenty and sixty assembled nuclear weapons, according to various estimates by experts" (Eleanor Albert, "North Korea's Military Capabilities," Council on Foreign Relations, September 5, 2017). See also Roh Suk-jo, "N.Korea 'Could Have 30–40 Nukes Next Year,'" *Chosun Ilbo*, September 17, 2019.

[3]   North Korea never admits or offers to drop its far greater hostility toward the United States.

nuclear weapons beyond such protections as missile defenses instituted to deal with the other North Korean military threats. This is despite the fact that it now seems clear that Kim will not give up his nuclear weapons and is instead committed to a nuclear weapon buildup.[4]

The ROK and the United States have not built the capabilities to counter the existing North Korean nuclear weapon threat. Because it usually takes years to develop such capabilities, we focus our analysis on the threat that North Korea might pose in the mid to late 2020s (using 2027 as our target year). We explain why North Korea is pursuing a large nuclear weapon force, why that matters, and what can be done about it. The community of experts on Korea recognizes that North Korea has already built a nuclear weapon force of dozens of nuclear weapons,[5] and our analysis indicates that the North might be able to produce about 200 nuclear weapons and hundreds of ballistic missiles for delivery by roughly 2027, enough to give the North what it might perceive as a nuclear force capable of enabling peninsula dominance. This would be a serious threat to the ROK and the United States. No one wants a nuclear war with North Korea that could cause millions of deaths and serious injuries and massive physical damage. The best way to avoid such a war is to prepare for it and demonstrate to North Korea that it cannot win such a conflict, even if it uses nuclear weapons. This was the perspective offered by Roman general Vegetius when he wrote: "If you want peace, prepare for war."[6] The ROK and the United States need to take action now to deter North Korean nuclear weapon use, to prepare for defeating that use should deterrence fail, and to induce North Korea to reduce its nuclear weapon threat.

Trapped by the Kim Family Legacy and North Korean Reality

The North Korean regime apparently feels trapped by its legacy and by current conditions in Korea, forcing it into a fundamental dependence on nuclear weapons. Kim Il-sung is still deified and revered as having godlike status, making Kim family policies extraordinarily difficult to change. In his final instructions to his son Kim Jong-un, Kim Jong-il provided 44 directives, several of which were particularly vital:

> The continuous development and procurement of nuclear weapons, long-range ballistic missiles, and chemical biological weapons is the only way to preserve

---

[4]   North Korean leader Kim Jong-un has made many statements to this effect, including recently, at the Eighth Party Congress in January 2021. See, for example, Choi Soo-hyang, "Kim Calls U.S. 'Principal Enemy,' Vows to Continue Nuclear Development," Yonhap News Agency, January 9, 2021.

[5]   See, for example, Hecker and Carlin, 2019.

[6]   Jack David, "Address: If You Want Peace, Prepare for War—U.S. Military Pre-Eminence and Why It Matters," Hudson Institute, March 8, 2014.

peace on the Korean Peninsula, and you must take this mission seriously and never lose sight of it.

We must unify Korea. The unification of the peninsula is the ultimate goal of our family. Even if we cannot accomplish this goal during Jung Eun's [Kim Jong-un's] generation, we must continue to strive for unification in future generations.

In order to do this, we must kick out the Americans from South Korea and we must overcome China's political and economic interjections in our domestic affairs.

It is important to maintain a good relationship with China. Although China is currently our closest partner nation, it's also a country that we should be most wary of in the future. Historically, China has been the country that has made us the most miserable.[7]

North Korea's poverty, corruption, and inefficiencies make these policies difficult to perform, especially for Kim Jong-un. In 2020, a combination of United Nations (UN) and U.S. sanctions, the coronavirus disease 2019 pandemic and the corresponding North Korea–initiated trade cutoff, and bad weather have contributed to Kim failing on many of his commitments to his people, creating conditions in which North Korean business failures and starvation are plaguing the North.[8] These conditions are combined with a serious inflow of outside information, and all of these factors could undermine Kim's control. Furthermore, China wishes to become a global hegemon by 2049,[9] with the potential to undermine the regime's control of the North.

Many Americans who are familiar with North Korea believe that, because of ROK and U.S. military superiority, the Kim family cannot militarily conquer the ROK and thereby control Korean unification.[10] Kim Jong-un's grandfather thought that there was another way: He thought he could decouple the ROK-U.S. alliance,[11] leaving the ROK vulnerable to absorption. But Kim Jong-un likely realizes that such a full Korean unification would deluge the North with outside information and likely destabilize the North Korean regime. Instead, Kim apparently hopes to use his nuclear weapons to break the ROK-U.S. alliance and then coerce the ROK into some form of

---

[7] "김정일 유서 전문 [Full Text of Kim Jong-il's Will]," U Korea News, November 23, 2012 (text translated from Korean by Diana Myers, a member of the RAND staff). These instructions were widely reported in the ROK media (although mainly in Korean). In English, see, for example, Jeong Yong-soo, "Kim Jong-il's Final Orders: Build More Weapons," *JoongAng Daily*, January 29, 2013.

[8] "Residents of N. Korea's Embattled Cities Face Starvation amid Continuing Coronavirus Blockade," *Rimjin gang*, December 16, 2020.

[9] Hal Brands, "What Does China Really Want? To Dominate the World," *Japan Times*, May 22, 2020.

[10] This observation is based upon dozens of conversations by the U.S. authors with personnel in the U.S. national security and Korea expert community.

[11] Don Oberdorfer, *The Two Koreas: A Contemporary History*, New York: Basic Books, 1997, p. 94.

confederation in which the North dominates the ROK. The North would use this confederation to exploit the economic wealth of the ROK but still maintain tight control over the flow of information to North Koreans.[12] However, this approach would still be extremely risky to Kim.

Kim's nuclear program is his one real success and the key to unification, making it essentially impossible for him to negotiate dismantlement of that program as he has promised. Indeed, it is not clear that Kim can perform any real denuclearization by halting nuclear weapon production or destroying nuclear weapons. Instead, he has done exactly the opposite, building more nuclear weapons and increasing his capabilities to build nuclear weapons.[13] He will likely need about 200 nuclear weapons to achieve his objectives; therefore, in this piece, we focus on North Korean efforts to build such a force of nuclear weapons in the coming decade and what the ROK and the United States should do about it.

Organization of This Perspective

The rest of this Perspective is divided into four chapters.[14] In Chapter Two, we discuss North Korean objectives and the role that nuclear weapons appear to play in supporting those objectives. In Chapter Three, we describe the potential sizes and characteristics of North Korea's nuclear weapon forces and the associated ballistic missiles. In Chapter Four, we postulate how North Korea has used its nuclear weapons for coercive and other purposes in peacetime and how it likely would use its nuclear weapons in a limited or major conflict. Finally, in Chapter Five, we offer recommendations on what the ROK and the United States can do in an effort to rein in the North Korean nuclear weapon threat. We also discuss how these actions need to be coordinated with China because of Chinese influence in the region.

---

[12]   The logic of this approach to "unification" is described in Chapters Two and Four.

[13]   Courtney Kube, Ken Dilanian, and Carol E. Lee, "North Korea Has Increased Nuclear Production at Secret Sites, Say U.S. Officials," NBC News, last updated June 30, 2018.

[14]   The original draft of Chapter Two was written by Go Myong-hyun, with contributions by Bruce Klingner; that of Chapter Three was written by Bruce E. Bechtol, Jr., and Park Jiyoung; that of Chapter Four was written by Bruce Klingner and Cha Du Hyeogn; and that of Chapter Five was written by Bruce Bennett and Choi Kang.

North Korea's National Strategy: Looking Beyond Nuclear Capability

It is becoming increasingly evident that the most important driver of North Korea's national strategy is its nuclear and missile capability. After two years of toying with diplomacy, North Korea's leadership has apparently decided to revert to its default position of fomenting tension and issuing threats against the ROK-U.S. alliance in lieu of dialogue. The blowing-up of the Joint Liaison Office in the Kaesong Industrial Complex on June 16, 2020; the still-pending threat to dismantle the inter-Korean military agreement; and Kim Jong-un's reaffirmation of North Korea as a nuclear weapon state once again prove that North Korea is nowhere near embarking on the path of complete denuclearization, as it had promised to the world to do in the April 2018 Panmunjom Declaration and at the Singapore Summit in June 2018.[1] North Korea persists in wanting to be called a "nuclear weapon state," using that terminology in its constitution,[2] and wanting to be identified as a peer of the five nuclear weapon states in the nuclear Nonproliferation Treaty (NPT).[3] The NPT authorizes only these five states to possess nuclear weapons. Other countries with nuclear weapons, including North Korea, are usually referred to as *nuclear-armed states*.[4]

---

[1] In the 2018 Panmunjom Declaration, Kim and ROK President Moon Jae-in agreed to fully implement "all existing inter-Korean declarations and agreements adopted thus far" (Moon Jae-in and Kim Jong-un, Panmunjeom Declaration on Peace, Prosperity and Reunification of the Korean Peninsula, Panmunjom, South Korea, April 27, 2018). One of those declarations was the 1992 Denuclearization Declaration, in which the North and South committed not to "test, manufacture, produce, receive, possess, store, deploy or use nuclear weapons. The South and the North shall use nuclear energy solely for peaceful purposes. The South and the North shall not possess nuclear reprocessing and uranium enrichment facilities" (Chung Won-shik, Republic of Korea, and Yon Hyong-muk, Democratic People's Republic of Korea, Joint Declaration of the Denuclearization of the Korean Peninsula, January 20, 1992, p. 8).

[2] Mathew Ha, "Amended North Korean Constitution Reaffirms Kim Jong Un's Steadfast Faith in His Nuclear Arsenal," Foundation for Defense of Democracies, July 15, 2019.

[3] The five nuclear weapon states in the NPT are China, France, Russia, the United Kingdom, and the United States.

[4] In Korean, *nuclear weapon state* is written as 핵보유국. *Nuclear-armed state* is written as 핵무장국.

Although this state of affairs is not surprising, North Korea has used its status as a nuclear-armed state to seek designation as a nuclear weapon state. North Korea's aims in other areas would be achieved by leveraging its nuclear capability. Political and economic successes would trickle down from the success of North Korea's national strategy in military and diplomatic domains. Therefore, North Korea is placing priority on developing and showcasing its nuclear capability and parlaying its technical capability to objectives in the diplomatic domain.

This strategy makes technical development the top priority and preferred strategic path for the regime. The sooner that North Korea demonstrates its complete intercontinental ballistic missile (ICBM) capability, the easier it will be for the regime to achieve its national objectives. But this does not mean that North Korea's diplomatic efforts are misleading; one clear bottleneck in North Korea's quest for designation as a nuclear weapon state is the need for legitimization of its nuclear weapon possession by the United States.

At present, this is the step with which the regime is having difficulties. Having come tantalizingly close to achieving this legitimization from U.S. President Donald Trump, it failed to cajole him to be even more accommodating of North Korea. Although legitimization is yet to be realized, this is the key diplomatic step for the regime: After having legitimized its illicit nuclear ambition, North Korea would pursue acceptance of its inhumane and outdated political system and would eventually attempt to normalize relations with the economic powerhouses of the region on a basis that would be favorable to North Korea.

Ultimately, North Korea's goal is to be recognized as a regional great power. However, because North Korea has the smallest economy in the region, nuclear capability by itself is not enough for the country to attain its goal. It is the influence and leverage conferred by the nuclear state status that North Korea apparently hopes will allow it to extract economic concessions from its prosperous neighbors.

As a result, North Korea strives to have its possession of nuclear capability legitimized by the United States,[5] which would be the tipping point in its quest to become a regional great power. Its primacy over the ROK and the affairs of the Korean Peninsula would follow, and North Korea could eventually force the ROK to accept terms of unification that would be favorable to the North. A free and affluent ROK poses an existential threat to the North. The North Korean regime's long-term viability can be assured only if North Korea places the ROK completely under its sphere of influence.

---

[5]   Bae Sung-won, "김정은 '미북회담 목적은 핵보유국 인정'···하노이 회담 앞서 군부에 핵개발 지침 [Kim Jong Un 'The Goal of the U.S.-North Korean Summit Was to Be Recognized as an Official Nuclear State' . . . Military Nuclear Development Guidelines Ahead of the Hanoi Summit]," Voice of America, June 18, 2019.

Then, North Korea could finally become a "Strong and Prosperous Nation" (강성대국)[6] with a combination of nuclear might and economic prosperity—a regional great power.

North Korea's National Strategy

The National Goal: A "Strong and Prosperous Nation"

Although the shape of North Korea's national strategy is becoming more visible as the country accumulates more nuclear capability and the regime further displays its disdain for making concessions in the diplomatic process, the ROK and U.S. community of experts has long expressed the belief that North Korea's ultimate goal is not to become a nuclear-armed state but to monetize its capability.[7] The "Hollywood-style video"[8] that President Trump showed Kim at the Singapore summit, in which he gently nudged Kim to exercise "vision and leadership" to take his country onto the path toward economic prosperity in lieu of nuclear armament, is yet another display of this (mistaken) belief.

This conception of North Korea's national strategy—that its ultimate objective is financial or diplomatic payoffs through nuclear blackmail rather than power and influence—rested on a rather dismissive view of North Korea and its regime.[9] To a degree, North Korea has even used such a scornful attitude held by the international community to its advantage by obfuscating its true motivation and obtaining assistance from friends and foes alike.[10]

The regime's public statements since 2010 have always reaffirmed its commitment to nuclear possession. Recent intelligence assessments and regime statements argue that the regime will never give up all of its nuclear weapons or infrastructure. The U.S. Intelligence Community assesses that "North Korea is unlikely to give up all of its nuclear weapons and production capabilities, even as it seeks to negotiate partial denuclearization steps to obtain key US and international concessions."[11] Pyongyang has declared that it will never abandon its nuclear arsenal and that "only fools will

---

[6]   Ministry of Unification of South Korea, "Korea Institute for National Unification Dictionary," webpage, December 31, 2016.

[7]   Graham T. Allison, Jr., "North Korea's Lesson: Nukes for Sale," *New York Times*, February 12, 2013.

[8]   Saba Hamedy, "President Trump Showed Kim Jong Un This Hollywood-Style Video to Pitch Him on Peace," CNN, June 12, 2018.

[9]   Shane Smith, *North Korea's Evolving Nuclear Strategy*, Washington, D.C.: US-Korea Institute at SAIS, August 2015a.

[10]   Joseph S. Nye, Jr., "North Korea's Powerful Weakness," *Project Syndicate*, July 11, 2013.

[11]   Daniel R. Coats, Director of National Intelligence, "Worldwide Threat Assessment of the US Intelligence Community," statement presented before the U.S. Senate Select Committee on Intelligence on January 29, 2019, Washington, D.C.: Office of the Director of National Intelligence, 2019, p. 27.

entertain the delusion that we will trade our nuclear deterrent for petty economic aid."[12] The Central Committee of the Korean Workers' Party affirmed that the country's nuclear weapons "are not goods for getting U.S. dollars and they are not a political bargaining chip."[13] Pyongyang's nuclear arsenal provides a "trusted shield"[14] and "treasured sword"[15] to support both defensive and offensive missions.

Regime nuclear weapons concurrently fulfill several domestic, foreign policy, and military objectives, which we discuss in the following subsections. As a result, nuclear weapons are indispensable assets to the Kim regime.

Provide Leadership Legitimacy

Lacking the revolutionary credentials and lengthy government tenure of his predecessors, Kim has linked his personal prestige and legitimacy as leader to maintaining the heritage of his father and grandfather and, in particular, to sustaining and maturing North Korea's nuclear and missile programs. He elevated the importance and visibility of these programs and embraced the breakthroughs of recent years as his exclusive contribution to defending the country. North Korean official media frequently release photos of Kim attending missile launches, lauding him as the visionary and driving force of innovation and success in North Korea.

Preserve the Kim Regime and the Nation

Pyongyang justifies its nuclear weapons as guaranteed protection against the U.S. "hostile policy" of military attacks and regime change against authoritarian regimes. Kim brags that his nuclear force constitutes "a powerful deterrent that prevents [the United States] from starting an adventurous war. In no way would the United States dare to ignite a war against me and our country."[16] In saying so, Kim mirrors U.S. efforts to protect the ROK against a North Korean invasion from 1958 until 1991, deploying up to 950 nuclear weapons in the ROK.[17] During this time, the U.S. nuclear weapon threat deterred major North Korean aggression, an irksome development for North Korea but also a useful example. North Korea points to U.S. and international interventions in Yugoslavia, Iraq, Libya, and Syria, as well as Russia's incursion into

---

[12] "North Korea Pledges Not to Abandon Nukes," AsiaOne, February 21, 2010.

[13] "2013 Plenary Meeting of WPK Central Committee and 7th Session of Supreme People's Assembly," North Korea Economy Watch, April 1, 2013.

[14] "N. Korea Says No Plans to Give Up Nuclear Capabilities," Yonhap News Agency, May 28, 2013.

[15] Josh Smith, "'Treasured Sword': North Korea Seen as Reliant as Ever on Nuclear Arsenal as Talks Stall," Reuters, November 13, 2018.

[16] Joshua Keating, "Kim and Trump Don't Mean the Same Thing When They Talk About 'Denuclearization,'" *Slate*, March 28, 2018.

[17] Hans M. Kristensen and Robert S. Norris, "A History of US Nuclear Weapons in South Korea," *Bulletin of the Atomic Scientists*, Vol. 73, No. 6, 2017.

Ukraine, as evidence of the necessity of nuclear weapons to prevent an attack on North Korea.

In reality, the principal threat to North Korean regime survival is from inside North Korea, because of the failures and brutality of the North Korean regime.[18] Nuclear weapons also help Kim deal with these inside threats by making him appear to be successful and powerful and, therefore, a fit leader of the North Korean people. And if North Korea unifies the Korean people under the North's control, Kim will appear to be even more powerful and successful.

Establish North Korea as a Regional Great Power

For internal political purposes, Kim wants North Korea to appear to be a regional great power, with him as its exalted leader. Kim seeks the following:

1. ensure regime survival and maintain absolute control over North Korea
2. achieve peninsula dominance—i.e., Korean unification of some form under regime control
3. make North Korea a regional great power that is able to achieve the first two objectives and to thwart even domination by the United States and China.

He sought to hold summit meetings with President Trump, giving Kim the opportunity to declare that he is a peer of the U.S. President. This is an example of how Kim has made North Korea a revisionist regional country seeking to redress decades of Japanese occupation followed by U.S. domination.[19] By making North Korea appear (at least internally) to be a nuclear armed state and a peer of the United States, Kim seeks to make his regime appear to be a success, demonstrating his ability to overcome the North's own "century of humiliation." Kim's aspiration to have dozens of nuclear-armed ICBMs would give him the ability to contest U.S. nuclear dominance by threatening nuclear attack on the United States in response to any nuclear attack on North Korea. Indeed, in the Eighth Party Congress, held in January 2021, Kim said, "Our external political activities must focus on controlling and subjugating the United States, our archenemy and the biggest stumbling block to the development of

---

[18] Thae Yong-Ho, member of the National Assembly of the Republic of Korea, "The Korean Peninsula Issues and US National Security," virtual address to Institute for Corean-American Studies, ICAS Winter Symposium, December 17, 2020.

[19] The U.S. 2018 National Defense Strategy characterizes China and Russia as revisionist powers but North Korea as a rogue regime. In doing so, it says: "North Korea seeks to guarantee regime survival and increased leverage by seeking a mixture of nuclear, biological, chemical, conventional, and unconventional weapons and a growing ballistic missile capability to gain coercive influence over South Korea, Japan, and the United States" (U.S. Department of Defense, *Summary of the 2018 National Defense Strategy of the United States of America: Sharpening the American Military's Competitive Edge*, Washington, D.C., 2018a, p. 2). The magnitude of the increased leverage that North Korea seeks makes it clearly both a rogue and a revisionist power.

our revolution."[20] The North Korean threat of a nuclear attack on U.S. homeland cities might be sufficient leverage for North Korea to break the U.S. nuclear umbrella and perhaps even the ROK-U.S. alliance (see the next subsection), allowing North Korean dominance of the ROK. Kim also knows that China plans to become a global hegemon in the next few decades, and Kim needs some major strength that he can use to reduce the influence that China likely will try to apply to North Korea. Kim apparently aspires to return North Korea to regional great-power status, a status experienced by some of the historical Korean dynasties, such as Koguryeo.

Moreover, Kim is sensitive to the fact that the ROK sits directly next to North Korea and demonstrates a much better life, forcing him to try to prevent much ROK information from coming into North Korea.[21] North Korea has always been afraid of a free and affluent ROK, because it represents a far more attractive model of national success than North Korea's oppressive and paranoid ideology. So long as the ROK stands as the shining city on a hill for the Korean nation, the regime's legitimacy will always be questioned, which will persist unless the North places the ROK completely under its control through unification.[22] As North Korean expert Andrei Lankov has said of North Korea, "Isolation is a condition of survival."[23] Indeed, the North does not want to legitimize the ROK government through much negotiation or cooperation, fearing that doing so would (1) raise questions about North Korean constitutional claims of sovereignty over the entire peninsula and (2) make the ROK a viable alternative to the North Korean regime, one that many in the North would see as a better alternative.

Decouple the ROK-U.S. Alliance

Pyongyang's increasing ability to target the continental United States with nuclear weapons has aggravated allies' concerns about the capability, resolve, and willingness of the United States to defend its allies. North Korea seeks to erode the credibility of the U.S. extended deterrence guarantee by sowing doubt as to whether Washington would come to allies' defense once the U.S. homeland is under nuclear threat.

North Korea seeks to drive a wedge between the United States and the ROK by depicting Seoul's alliance with Washington and "nuclear war exercises" as a *casus belli*

---

[20]   Choe Sang-Hun, "Kim Jong-un Vows to Boost North Korea's Nuclear Capability as Leverage with Biden," *New York Times*, last updated January 15, 2021b.

[21]   North Korean security services can impose prison sentences for those caught with DVDs or USBs containing ROK soap operas or other media. However, in practice, the corruption of the security services generally leads people to offer significant bribes to the security personnel to avoid prison. See, for example, Jieun Baek, "Why Foreign Information in North Korea Is Such a Big Deal," NK News, October 19, 2016.

[22]   Choi Kang, "Concerned About the Korean Version of 'Stockholm Syndrome,'" *Chosun Ilbo*, January 19, 2021.

[23]   Andrei Lankov and Wang Son-taek, "Is the Dream of Korean Reunification Dead?" NK News Podcast Ep. 162, December 24, 2020.

and to compel the latter to stay on the sidelines in the case of a conflict.[24] In 2017, Ri Jong-hyok, deputy of the Supreme People's Assembly of North Korea, commented, "Our nuclear deterrence is a sword of justice aimed at fighting [U.S. nuclear weapons, and] any country in the world need not worry about our threats as long as they do not join [the] invasion and provocations toward us."[25]

Enhance Coercive Diplomacy

Attaining an unambiguous nuclear ICBM capability could lead Pyongyang to perceive that it has immunity from any international response—and thus lead the regime to act even more belligerently and to seek to intimidate the United States and its allies into accepting North Korean diktats. Pyongyang could use nuclear weapons to coerce the ROK to request reduced U.S. force levels and an end to bilateral military exercises. The regime could use threats of nuclear attack to intimidate Tokyo to preclude U.S. forces from using Japanese bases, ports, and airfields during a Korean conflict.

Augment Warfighting Capability

An iconic Korean proverb that depicts the peninsula as surrounded by larger enemies says that "when the whales fight, it is the shrimp's back that is broken." Nuclear weapons enable the "shrimp" to fend off the much larger "whales." They are the great equalizer.

Nuclear weapons deter allied preemptive or decapitation attacks, inhibit allied military responses to North Korean actions, degrade allied invasion plans, threaten the U.S. homeland, and potentially provide the means for Pyongyang to reunify the peninsula on its terms.

Nuclear weapons also could provide the ultimate act of defiance amid a collapsing regime—the *Götterdämmerung* ("twilight of the gods"), or Samson collapsing the temple down upon himself. In 1993, Kim Il-sung convened his generals to ask them what they would do if the United States attacked and North Korea lost the war. When the generals hesitated, presumably unwilling to acknowledge the potential for loss, Kim Jong-il arose and exclaimed, "I will be sure to destroy the Earth! What good is this Earth without North Korea?"[26]

The scope and totality of North Korea's nuclear arsenal enable the regime to punch far above its strategic weight class, and there should be no ambiguity over North Korea's intention to keep its nuclear capability. The international community's initial mistake was to assume that North Korea's nuclear weapons were no big deal and were only a bargaining chip. But now that North Korea's strategic leverage is based heav-

---

[24] See, for example, "N. Korean FM Claims U.S. Nuclear Threats Result in Pyongyang's Nuclear Development," *Korea Times*, April 21, 2016.

[25] "Senior N. Korean Official Says Its Nuke Program Targets No Country But U.S.," Yonhap News Agency, November 26, 2017.

[26] Kim Hyun Sik, "The Secret History of Kim Jong Il," *Foreign Policy*, October 6, 2009.

ily on nuclear possession, the opposite mistake is being made by the international community—that is, assuming that North Korea's nuclear strategy is its national strategy. Although North Korea's nuclear strategy is the centerpiece of its national strategy, its nuclear strategy is still the means to an end—and North Korea's most desired end is to make the country a "Strong and Prosperous Nation."

The concept of a "Strong and Prosperous Nation" is not mere sloganeering. It consists of a vision of North Korea that is engaged in constant struggles but comes out victorious by becoming, in stages, a political-ideological power, a military power, and, finally, an economic power.[27] The concept is also a legacy of Kim Jong-il that has been elevated to national strategic vision by Kim Jong-un. North Korea will leverage its nuclear capability to achieve the national goal of becoming a strong and prosperous nation. Arguably, North Korea is at the cusp of completing the second stage of its vision, which is to be designated as a nuclear weapon state. The question for North Korea is how to attain its ultimate objective of becoming economically prosperous.

The Key Driver: North Korea's Nuclear Arsenal

In this chapter, we argue that North Korean nuclear weapons are the key means for accomplishing North Korea's national strategy, which is to develop nukes, build many of them, diversify their yields and sizes, and field a variety of delivery systems that have the range to reach the continental United States. More nuclear weapons would give North Korea a wider set of options. Although North Korea has yet to announce its official nuclear doctrine, there is little doubt that its future nuclear posture will closely correspond to the number of warheads that it will deploy. For instance, Choi and Kim argue that North Korea's nuclear doctrine will evolve along with its nuclear capability, going from a relatively defensive posture of assured retaliation to a more aggressive asymmetric escalation as its nuclear forces become more powerful and capable.[28]

In fact, there are strong indications that North Korea is currently engaged in a race to enlarge and diversify its nuclear arsenal. North Korea may have restrained itself from carrying out provocations in 2018 and 2019 not because it was giving diplomacy a chance, but rather because its strategy had shifted from testing to mass production of nuclear weapons.[29] North Korea is expected to have amassed up to 100 nuclear warheads by 2020.[30] North Korea is also accelerating the production of ICBMs and

---

[27]   Ministry of Unification of South Korea, 2016.

[28]   Choi Kang and Kim Gibum, "A Thought on North Korea's Nuclear Doctrine," *Korean Journal of Defense Analysis*, Vol. 29, No. 4, December 2017.

[29]   Alexander Smith, "North Korea Launched No Missiles in 2018. But That Isn't Necessarily Due to Trump," NBC News, last updated December 31, 2018.

[30]   Gian Gentile, Yvonne K. Crane, Dan Madden, Timothy M. Bonds, Bruce W. Bennett, Michael J. Mazarr, and Andrew Scobell, *Four Problems on the Korean Peninsula: North Korea's Expanding Nuclear Capabilities Drive a Complex Set of Problems*, Santa Monica, Calif.: RAND Corporation, TL-271-A, 2019.

transporter-erector-launchers (TELs), as evidenced by the report on the Sil-li ballistic missile support facility, which can accommodate the large Hwasong-15 ICBM.[31]

If North Korea increases the quantity and capability of its nuclear forces, it would certainly be possible for North Korea to entertain the idea of employing a first use of nuclear weapons, perhaps with a tactical nuclear weapon to dissuade its enemies from engaging in further escalation.[32] With the development of the Sinpo-class ballistic missile submarine, North Korea claims that it will have developed a credible second-strike capability, although the Sinpo-class submarine likely would be vulnerable to attack while at sea. In fact, during a meeting of the Central Committee of the Korean Workers' Party in 2019,[33] Kim Jong-un had threatened to showcase a "new strategic weapon," which, after the North's military parade on October 10, 2020, appears to be a new, large ICBM.[34]

The rapid expansion of North Korea's nuclear weapon capability despite the external pressures of economic sanctions proves that nuclear weapons are the dominant parameter in the regime's strategy. North Korea is betting that once it amasses a sufficient nuclear arsenal with matching delivery capability, its main opponents—the United States, the ROK, and Japan—will be forced to accommodate its ambitious goals.

And history has shown that nuclear weapon development is one key variable that the international community has not been able to affect in North Korea's strategic calculations. The international community so far has tried to isolate North Korea diplomatically, politically, and economically, but its nuclear program has only advanced further. Nuclear development is not the weak link in North Korea's pursuit of national strategy. On the contrary, it is its bedrock.

The Critical Domain: Diplomacy

However, there is also a significant risk for North Korea in executing its strategy: It could stagnate as a nuclear-armed state while neighboring states deploy deterrence measures that could nullify its nuclear offensive capabilities. Regionwide missile defense systems, precision weaponry, and redeployment of tactical nuclear weapons by the United States are all responses that would undermine North Korea's nuclear advantage.

---

[31] Joseph S. Bermudez, Jr., "Sil-li Ballistic Missile Support Facility," Beyond Parallel, Center for Strategic and International Studies, May 5, 2020.

[32] Smith, 2015b, pp. 20–21.

[33] julesyi@yna.co.kr, "New Satellite Images Show N. Korea's Hidden Submarine Capable of Firing Ballistic Missiles," Yonhap News Agency, January 6, 2020.

[34] See NK News, "North Korea Military Parade 2020—Livestream & Analysis," video, YouTube, October 10, 2020, starting at about 2:08:00.

To avoid being trapped with nuclear weapons in a corner of Northeast Asia, North Korea would have to resort to diplomacy to maximize the influence and power that come from possessing nuclear weapons. This is the continuation of a preexisting pattern: North Korea's diplomacy has always been subservient to its nuclear and missile development roadmap and functioned as the off-ramp when North Korea's cycle of provocations became untenable. As U.S. Senator John Kerry put it,

> We need to find a way to break North Korea's cycle—and it is a cycle—of provocation and nuclear expansion, in which they kind of flex their muscles, then move back; they challenge us, we get slightly engaged, something happens, and we go back through the cycle again.[35]

North Korea employs diplomacy to trap its opponents in a never-ending "cycle of provocation and nuclear expansion" and prevent them from mounting effective counterresponses. This is also the definition of *gray zone strategy*: keeping the conflict below the threshold of major war, thereby forcing a much larger opponent to negotiate.[36] Now that North Korea has reached a critical pace and level of its cycle of nuclear weapon expansion, the biggest hurdle that it currently faces is the need to cement the gains accrued so far by having its nuclear capability tacitly legitimized by the United States. North Korea appears to perceive that this could be achieved as simply as by normalizing bilateral relations and signing a peace treaty despite North Korea's existing nuclear arsenal.

This necessity for legitimization is constant regardless of whether China and Russia support North Korea's ambitions. North Korea aspires to achieve full strategic autonomy from all major powers, and, historically, it has been able to be in charge of relations with its bigger allies.[37] North Korea is unlikely to sacrifice its goal for the sake of its ad hoc alliance with China and Russia.

However, the fact that diplomacy is the critical chokehold for the realization of North Korea's national strategy creates opportunities for the United States and its allies. The need for diplomatic legitimization on the part of North Korea is a powerful form of leverage that the United States unwittingly possesses over Kim's regime. The United States should disabuse itself of the notion that diplomatic normalization is a throwaway that is useful only in catalyzing negotiations with Pyongyang.

---

[35]   John F. Kerry, "Breaking the Cycle of North Korean Provocations," opening statement presented before the U.S. Senate Committee on Foreign Relations on March 1, 2011, Washington, D.C.: U.S. Government Printing Office, 2011.

[36]   Lyle J. Morris, Michael J. Mazarr, Jeffrey W. Hornung, Stephanie Pezard, Anika Binnendijk, and Marta Kepe, *Gaining Competitive Advantage in the Gray Zone: Response Options for Coercive Aggression Below the Threshold of Major War*, Santa Monica, Calif.: RAND Corporation, RR-2942-OSD, 2019.

[37]   Cheng Xiaohe, "The Evolution of Sino-North Korean Relations in the 1960s," *Asian Perspective*, Vol. 34, No. 2, 2010.

North Korea's Desired Path to Victory

Having discussed the three tenets of North Korea's strategy—the goal, key driver, and the critical domain—we can proceed to describe its national strategy, which we do in Table 2.1. Structurally, North Korea's strategy is composed of two levels, and military-diplomatic strategies and goals are placed above economic-political objectives. North Korea's economic-political objectives are subsumed into the larger military-diplomatic strategy that the regime pursues; the regime appears to believe that its economic-political goals will be accomplished once its primary goals have been accomplished. The dotted line that bisects the table into upper and lower sections denotes the hierarchical relationship between the military-diplomatic and economic-political domains.

Table 2.1 includes a wide variety of objectives and strategic steps that North Korea is employing to achieve its objective of becoming a regional great power. As the regime's nuclear and missile capabilities progress and its intermediate diplomatic goals are met (i.e., moving from left to right in the table), more options will open up to it. For example, North Korea will have the option of using nuclear coercion while also keeping the gray zone strategy in its portfolio of policy options.

The critical phases in North Korea's national strategy are the boxes marked 1, 2, and 3. These boxes are numbered in the order of North Korea's strategic execution. Stage 4 is the final phase; it represents North Korea's "victory" of becoming a "Strong and Prosperous Nation." Therefore, the most critical phase is Stage 2 (shaded red) of the diplomatic domain.

Nuclear capability, which is the key driver behind North Korea's national strategy and imbues it with credibility, is represented by the gray arrow. The nuclear development roadmap is unaffected by external pressure and acts as the pacemaker for North Korea's national strategy. The roadmap is parameterized by the number of nuclear warheads that North Korea possesses at a given moment. In 2020, the best estimates of North Korea's nuclear capability put the size of North Korea's nuclear arsenal at somewhere between 50 and 100 nuclear warheads.

When North Korea inevitably acquires more nuclear warheads, it will be able to spread them around for better survivability and second-strike capability. North Korea's ambitions and objectives will greatly expand when its relatively large nuclear arsenal is coupled with long-range ballistic missiles. North Korea likely hopes that, once the number of warheads reaches 200, potentially by 2027 (see Chapter Three), the international community will have no choice but to accept North Korea as a nuclear weapon state. The question is whether North Korea also will be allowed to impose its political and economic designs on the ROK and other neighboring countries.

The Status Quo and the Tipping Point

In the schematic of Table 2.1, the status quo is described in Box 1, "Nuclear Brinkmanship Diplomacy (Phase 1)." It corresponds to the current state of impasse: Despite the

Table 2.1
Evolution of North Korea's National Objectives Inferred by Nuclear and Missile System Developments

Domain	Evolving Situation	Objective
Nuclear status	Number of warheads: 50–100[a] Delivery system: MRBMs, IRBMs, and SLBMs	Number of warheads: about 200[b] Delivery system: MIRVed ICBMs and TBMs
Military	**Deterrence by Assured Retaliation** • Develop ICBM capability • Ensure second-strike capability with SLBMs on ballistic missile submarines **Hybrid Warfare** • Enhance long-range strike capability and reduce conventional forces • Enhance information warfare capability	**Nuclear-Armed Status** • Fully deploy dozens of MIRVed ICBMs • Dissolve extended deterrence and ROK-U.S. alliance • Exercise A2/AD strategy against U.S. intervention in the environs of the Korean Peninsula
Diplomatic	**Nuclear Brinkmanship Diplomacy (Phase 1)** • Entangle United States in "denuclearization" diplomatic quagmire by obfuscating North Korea's true intention • Gain international respect for North Korea and perception that it is no longer a failed state **Nuclear Brinkmanship Diplomacy (Phase 2)** • Force United States to accept "gradual path toward denuclearization" • Have the United States and North Korea enter into peace talks • Normalize diplomatic relations with United States • Partially dismantle old sites to induce United States to lift sanctions	**Regional Great-Power Status** • Achieve U.S.–North Korea peace treaty • Achieve withdrawal or minimization of U.S. Forces Korea • Achieve bilateral arms-control talks • Obtain U.S. assurance that it will intervene in Korean Peninsula affairs only with North Korea's prior consent • Achieve strategic autonomy from China, Russia • Achieve full lifting of sanctions
Economic	**The New Path (Phase 1)** • Accept dependence on China's assistance and strategic support • Implement structural adjustments to withstand economic pressure **The New Path (Phase 2)** • Achieve partial lifting of sanctions • Restart inter-Korean economic engagement • Make China and Russia more emboldened to assist North Korea	**Parasitic Exploitation** • Compel ROK, China, and Japan to enter into preferential trade and investment agreements with the North • Rebuild public distribution system and centrally planned economy

Table 2.1—Continued

Domain	Evolving Situation		Objective
Political	**Prestige and Propaganda (Phase 1)** • Strengthen Kim Jong-un's legitimacy and consolidate control • Gain international respect for North Korea and perception that it is no longer a failed state: e.g., U.S.–North Korea summits	**Prestige and Propaganda (Phase 2)** • Fully attain international respect through normalization of diplomatic relations with United States and Japan • Increase public favorability by partial lifting of sanctions and restart of inter-Korean economic engagement	**One State, Two Systems** • Compel ROK to legalize communist parties • Intervene in ROK politics and foreign policy through proxy parties • Make ROK North Korea's protectorate[c]

NOTES: A2/AD = anti-access/area denial; IRBM = intermediate-range ballistic missile; MIRV = multiple independent reentry vehicle; MRBM = medium-range ballistic missile; SLBM = submarine-launched ballistic missile; TBM = theatre ballistic missile. The gray arrow in the second row represents nuclear capability. The boxes marked 1, 2, and 3 are the critical phases in North Korea's national strategy; these boxes are numbered in the order of North Korea's strategic execution. The red box represents Stage 2 of the diplomatic domain—the most critical phase. The box marked 4 is the final phase and represents North Korea's "victory." Gray boxes represent desired end states; these result when items above and items to the left are achieved.

[a] It is assumed that North Korea has at least 50 warheads as of 2020.

[b] Estimated number of warheads in 2027.

[c] Actual unification is too risky.

breakdown of talks in Hanoi, Vietnam, in 2019, the United States is still entangled in a diplomatic dead end with North Korea. Although North Korea did not cross the Trump administration's implicit redline of ICBM testing,[38] it did launch a mix of 25 advanced short-range ballistic missiles in 2019 and another nine in 2020,[39] indicating that North Korea is still engaged in the development of delivery means.

The Trump administration was focused on sustaining peace in the face of the intractable nature of North Korean denuclearization.[40] Pyongyang's relentless production of nuclear weapons was taking place while President Trump was prioritizing his personal relationship with Kim,[41] despite the failure of the Hanoi Summit. President Trump's focus on personal diplomacy was raising concern that he could cut a deal with Kim for the deal's sake,[42] but that did not happen.

If the U.S. government were to opt for dialogue over pressure, North Korea will have advanced from the status quo (Box 1) to the second phase of its diplomatic initiative (Box 2). North Korea could even offer to dismantle a number of old nuclear sites in exchange for U.S. concessions, as it did in the Hanoi Summit when it proposed shutting down the Yongbyon nuclear sites in exchange for a substantial lifting of sanctions.

The lack of progress will eventually lead the United States to explore a more gradual approach toward negotiating with North Korea.[43] Advocates of a softer, gradualist approach even suggest that the United States should unilaterally sign a peace treaty with the North and establish a diplomatic presence in Pyongyang.[44] Alas, this is exactly what Senator Kerry described as a trap in North Korea's provocation cycle: After a period of escalation, North Koreans take a step back and the two sides enter

---

[38]   Bruce W. Bennett, "Stability in Northeast Asia and the North Korean 'Christmas Present,'" *RAND Blog*, December 24, 2019.

[39]   Nuclear Threat Initiative, CNS North Korea Missile Test Database, October 16, 2020; and UN Security Council, *Final Report of the Panel of Experts Submitted Pursuant to Resolution 2464*, New York, S/2020/151, March 2, 2020, pp. 69–71.

[40]   The United States accepted a de facto freeze-for-freeze arrangement in early 2018. Kim promised to suspend his missile and nuclear weapon tests, and the ROK and the United States pulled back from President Trump's maximum-pressure campaign and suspended military exercises until after the winter Olympic Games in the ROK. See International Crisis Group, *The Korean Peninsula Crisis (II): From Fire and Fury to Freeze-for-Freeze*, Brussels, Belgium, Asia Report No. 294, January 23, 2018.

[41]   Shim Kyu-seok, "North Korea Scoffs at Another Summit with Trump," *JoongAng Daily*, July 5, 2020.

[42]   David E. Sanger and Choe Sang-Hun, "Two Years After Trump-Kim Meeting, Little to Show for Personal Diplomacy," *New York Times*, June 12, 2020. Many experts on North Korea sought to create a meaningful agreement with North Korea before President Trump would meet with Kim. However, according to a colleague at the State Department, the North Koreans never allowed their nuclear weapon experts to meet with the U.S. negotiators; thus, it was impossible to establish the technical details that would be needed to get even a meaningful first step toward North Korean denuclearization.

[43]   Baik Sung-won, "Experts: Step-by-Step Approach Needed in Denuclearization Deal with North Korea," Voice of America, June 25, 2019b.

[44]   James Clapper, "Ending the Dead End in North Korea," *New York Times*, May 19, 2018.

into negotiations, which allows North Korea to consolidate the gains of nuclear expansion in exchange for de-escalating tension.

The fear, then, is less about North Korea becoming a nuclear-armed state than about a sitting U.S. President legitimizing North Korea's nuclear and missile capabilities without implementing complete, verifiable, and irreversible dismantlement (CVID) denuclearization. Such an acknowledgment would entail normalization of relations and complete or partial lifting of sanctions, and it would constitute the tipping point in North Korea's national strategy. From that point onward, North Korea would be able to parlay its nuclear capability not only into strengthening its deterrence but also into imposing its political will on its opponents.

The phase that follows the tipping point is the point of no return (Box 4 in the table). North Korea appears to believe that being formally acknowledged by the United States as a nuclear-armed state would make it a de facto regional great power, able to impose its strategic and political designs on its neighbors, especially the ROK. This is a short stop away from being a "Strong and Prosperous Nation."

The Point of No Return

It is widely suspected that North Korea's conception of denuclearization does not entail CVID, but rather arms-control negotiations with the United States.[45] In fact, North Korea's definition of Korean Peninsula denuclearization requires that the United States not deploy strategic assets to the Korean Peninsula in exchange for nuclear arms reduction. This "regionwide denuclearization" also could involve removing the U.S. nuclear umbrella from Japan.[46]

A step-by-step, action-for-action denuclearization roadmap could lead not to North Korea's denuclearization, but to a general retreat of the U.S. presence from the region instead. North Korea would demand that the United States first sign a peace treaty, which could result in the dissolution of the UN Command (UNC), which acts as the backbone of the ROK's international defense.[47]

Even the normalization of relations with North Korea might not lead to lasting stability. North Korea practices coercive diplomacy by superseding provocations with harsh rhetoric until a deteriorating situation compels a much larger and powerful opponent to negotiate on equal terms.[48] This tactic is a powerful tool in North Korea's diplomatic toolbox, and the North is unlikely to give it up. In fact, as the prospect for

---

[45] Jo Sang-jin, "미 전문가들 "북한의 군축협상 시도 일축해야 [U.S. Experts Say, "North Korea's Military Disarmament Attempt Should Be Dismissed]," Voice of America, October 5, 2019.

[46] Anna Fifield, "North Korea's Definition of 'Denuclearization' Is Very Different from Trump's," *Washington Post*, April 9, 2018.

[47] In-Bum Chun, "The Future of the UN Command," 38 North, September 12, 2017.

[48] Yongho Kim, "North Korea's Use of Terror and Coercive Diplomacy: Looking for Their Circumstantial Variants," *Korean Journal of Defense Analysis*, Vol. 14, No. 1, 2002.

CVID denuclearization of North Korea becomes unlikely because of North Korea's intransigence and inconsistency in the U.S. approach, North Korea's demand for a mutual arms-control agreement is gaining more support.[49]

And it could get worse: Were the United States to legitimize a nuclear North Korea without ridding it of ICBMs and related infrastructure and technology, U.S. allies in the region and beyond would question the validity of U.S. extended deterrence.[50] Perception of a U.S. retreat from its defense commitment to the ROK could turn into reality even faster than expected. A recently published U.S. Army War College report, which was originally commissioned by then–U.S. Secretary of Defense Mark Esper, recommends that the U.S. Army readjust the mission profile of its forces stationed in Korea to fit the new Indo-Pacific strategy.[51] There is growing concern that the recommended adjustments would lead to a reduction of U.S. ground troops in the ROK.[52] This is a long-term Kim family objective: In the mid-1970s,

> Kim Il Sung was keenly aware of Carter's proposal to withdraw American troops from South Korea. Such a move had long been one of Kim's central goals, in the belief that this would lead inevitably to reuniting the peninsula under his leadership, whether by peaceful or violent means.[53]

The combination of a weakening of the U.S. defense commitment to the ROK, U.S. distraction caused by the growing strategic competition with China, and the domestic political exigencies of a fast peace with a recalcitrant enemy could lead to the empowerment of North Korea from a "mere" nuclear-armed state to a regional great power. North Korea would then move to establish its sphere of influence around the Korean Peninsula using its nuclear deterrence capability. It could even declare a North Korean version of the Monroe Doctrine: nonintervention by the United States in the environs of the Korean Peninsula.

North Korea's Goal and the ROK's Worst-Case Scenario: A "Strong and Prosperous Nation"

North Korea would establish itself as victor in the inter-Korean systemic competition after entering into an arms-control agreement and diplomatic normalization with the

---

[49] Baik, 2019b.

[50] Shane Smith, "Renewing US Extended Deterrence Commitments Against North Korea," 38 North, May 13, 2020.

[51] Nathan Freier, John Schaus, and William Braun, *An Army Transformed: USINDOPACOM Hypercompetition and US Army Theater Design*, Carlisle, Pa.: Strategic Studies Institute and US Army War College Press, 2020.

[52] Kim Dong-hyun, "미 전문가들, 주한미군 관련 육군대학원 보고서에 엇갈린 반응 [U.S. Experts: Report from the Army War College Provided Conflicting Perspectives on USFK]," Voice of America, July 31, 2020.

[53] Oberdorfer, 1997, p. 94.

United States. Rhetorically, the regime is already claiming victory. In 2018, North Korea claimed that it had developed nuclear weapons not to fight the ROK, but to ensure stability and peace for the entire Korean nation and the peninsula.[54] Still, this is not a sustainable outcome for North Korea unless the regime is able to solve the last piece of the puzzle: the mystery of economic development.

It is unlikely that North Korea will ever voluntarily engage in economic reform, even if its security fears are placated. If North Korea's nuclear capability is legitimized and its influence in the region tacitly acknowledged, North Korea will turn its focus toward the ROK, in part for ideological reasons. But the North also apparently realizes that only by leveraging its strategic superiority over the ROK will it achieve the downstream goal of resolving North Korea's intractable structural economic problems. North Korea is certain to demand ever-higher prices for keeping peace and stability on the Korean Peninsula, especially if it concludes that the ROK lacks strong deterrence against the North's nuclear capability. And the ROK's Pollyannaish attitude toward the North makes it a prime target for economic exploitation.

North Korea would seek economic prosperity by establishing an exploitative economic relationship with the ROK, and this task would be facilitated by the ROK's eagerness to throw money at the North. There is ample precedent for this: Despite Pyongyang's nuclear buildup, Seoul provided Pyongyang with around $930 million (U.S. dollars) in financial assistance between 2000 and 2008,[55] in addition to $1.4 billion worth of "humanitarian" assistance, which included food, fertilizers, and other materials.[56] The ROK is likely to allow the North to enjoy favorable terms of trade and cash transfusions camouflaged as "investments" in case a peace regime is established, even if it does not entail North Korea's denuclearization.[57] These would be justified as "peace dividends," because many in the ROK believe that it is cheaper to pay off the North than to keep the status quo of the divided peninsula.[58]

North Korea could replicate the model of a parasitic economic relationship with yet another neighboring country, Japan. Japan, like the ROK, is under the threat of North Korea's nuclear weapons, and the tacit legitimization of its nuclear capability by the United States might lead Japan to seek accommodation with North Korea. If

---

[54] Moon Kwan-hyun, "北통신 '핵무력, 동족 겨냥 아니다…철저히 미국 겨냥 [Nuclear Forces Are Not Targeted Toward Their Own People, It Is Surely for the United States]," Yonhap News Agency, February 24, 2018.

[55] Kim Dang, "단독] 대북 차관 1조617억원…北, 한푼도 안갚아 [Exclusive: Vice Minister of North Korea Did Not Pay Back Any of the 1 Trillion 61.7 Billion KRW in Loans to North Korea]," UPI News, June 19, 2020.

[56] At the current exchange rate (2020).

[57] John Dale Grover, "Engagement First: Why Some Koreans See Peacemaking and Peacebuilding as the Solution to North Korea," *National Interest*, May 11, 2020.

[58] Lee Jung-eun, "통일비용, 천문학적이라고?…전문가들 "분단비용 고려해야 [Unification Costs Are Astronomical? Experts Say Division of Costs Should Be Considered]," *Hankook-ilbo*, May 2, 2018.

the United States normalizes relations with North Korea, Japan is likely to follow suit soon after. However, unlike the United States, Japan will have to offer Pyongyang a significant reparation package for Japan's colonial misrule. In 2002, the last time such a negotiation took place, Japan considered giving North Korea an "economic assistance package" worth between $5 billion to $10 billion (U.S. dollars).[59] The size of the package today will have to be many times larger than the original offer, given inflation and North Korea's nuclear capability.

If North Korea normalizes relations with the United States, the partial lifting of sanctions is to be expected, which in turn would enable the North to enter into favorable trade and economic agreements with both the ROK and Japan. North Korea could then use these concessions as leverage to extract even more favorable economic benefits from China. China might continue or even expand the subsidized supply of crude and refined oil, as well as its import of North Korea's natural resources, to keep North Korea on its side. This is exactly where North Korea likes to position itself: balancing major powers against each other and strengthening its strategic autonomy in the process.

North Korea's enhanced strategic position would enable it to exercise even bigger influence on the ROK. The North would demand that the ROK either downgrade or altogether eliminate the ROK-U.S. alliance, which would be in peril in any case because of the tacit U.S. acknowledgment of North Korea as a nuclear-armed state. The North would also want the ROK to change its legal-political structure to transform an erstwhile pro–United States, globalized country into a more insular and nationalistic one. This could result in the repeal of the National Security Act and the legalization of the Communist party in the ROK. As the recent moves against defector activists by the ROK government show,[60] stifling of individual liberties for the sake of inter-Korean relations is no longer a far-fetched possibility. The transformation of the ROK to become more accommodating to the North would only accelerate if North Korea's nuclear capabilities were to gain international acceptance.

How to Undermine North Korea's National Strategy

Although letting North Korea gain a significant nuclear weapon force will have severe consequences, there is one critical weakness in North Korea's roadmap; in this chapter, we make a clear distinction between North Korea becoming a nuclear-armed state and North Korea being promoted as a regional great power. Although there is little that the

---

[59] Mark E. Manyin, *North Korea–Japan Relations: The Normalization Talks and the Compensation/Reparations Issue*, Washington, D.C.: Congressional Research Service, Library of Congress, RS20526, 2002.

[60] Jeongmin Kim and Kelly Kasulis, "South Korea Revokes Corporate License for Two Defector-Led Activist Groups," NK News, July 17, 2020.

United States and its allies can do to prevent the former,[61] the latter requires an explicit acknowledgment by the United States.

This implies that there is a fallacy in the current international community's efforts to prompt North Korea's denuclearization. Such efforts have focused primarily on coming up with a mutually agreeable denuclearization schedule with North Korea and have used diplomatic concessions (i.e., the Singapore and Hanoi summits) as catalysts for negotiating with North Korea.

We argue that that approach is exactly the opposite of what should be done. The United States should not "prime the pump" for dialogue with North Korea,[62] because unilateral concessions to the North seldom result in long-term reciprocity. The United States has already granted North Korea unilateral diplomatic concessions (i.e., two summit meetings and a third meeting with a sitting U.S. President)[63] and should avoid granting it any more, which could take the form of diplomatic recognition through normalization of relations, or the lifting of sanctions without demanding that North Korea demonstrate its commitment to a CVID denuclearization roadmap by freezing its nuclear weapon production and beginning to reduce its nuclear forces.

North Korea's national strategy is not complete unless its nuclear capability is tacitly acknowledged by the United States. Without this accommodation, North Korea will remain a serious threat, but also impoverished and limited in its regional influence. Therefore, the priority for the United States and its allies should be to minimize diplomatic concessions to the North while pressuring the regime to produce concrete information on its nuclear program to design an effective, intrusive inspection regimen when conditions permit.

Policymakers in Seoul, Washington, and elsewhere have fundamentally misunderstood North Korea's intention regarding its nuclear buildup. Nuclear weapons are not ancillary to its long-term strategy, but rather its bedrock. Therefore, the realistic option for countering the long-term North Korean threat is not "pie-in-the-sky" denuclearization, but rather containment by neutralizing North Korea's nuclear threat with massive deterrence measures.

North Korea is not going to abandon its nuclear weapons. Future ROK, U.S., and allied policies on North Korea should recognize this proven proposition. The response by the United States and the ROK should be to bolster deterrence credibility by (1) delaying the transfer of wartime operational control (OPCON) and (2) implementing ballistic missile defense and other forms of defense (see Chapter Five). How-

---

[61] It is believed that North Korea will respond only to military pressure in this regard.

[62] "[Editorial] S. Korea-US Joint Exercises Need to Be Delayed to Enable Bold Change in Inter-Korean Dialogue," *Hankyoreh*, July 22, 2020.

[63] In fairness, many experienced negotiators who had dealt with North Korea argued against President Trump meeting with Kim on the basis that simply meeting with a U.S. President is a valuable gift that should not be given away and that should have been used to secure meaningful North Korean denuclearization concessions.

ever, if these combined responses turn out to be unsuccessful, the ROK might need to consider developing and deploying indigenous nuclear weapon capabilities.

Faced with severe deterrence measures and the unlikelihood of its nuclear objectives ever being recognized and legitimized, North Korea's leaders eventually will realize that, instead of empowering them, nuclear weapons have trapped them in a little impoverished corner of Northeast Asia. Only then can the true denuclearization of North Korea begin.

CHAPTER THREE

North Korean Nuclear and Ballistic Missile Capabilities, Now and in 2027

North Korea's nuclear and ballistic missile capabilities have been for many years and continue to be top policy challenges for the United States and one of its key allies, the ROK. Not only are these two issues extremely important because of the threat that they present in the region, but now, with North Korea's demonstrated ICBM capability, these two issues (nuclear weapons and ballistic missiles as a platform to carry them) clearly present a real threat to the security of North Korea's neighbors, to the United States, and to its other allies around the world (through proliferation). But because it takes time (usually years) to develop counters, we focus on the threat that North Korea could likely pose in the late 2020s. (We use 2027 as our target date.)

This chapter addresses North Korea's nuclear weapons and ballistic missiles that likely would be used for nuclear weapon delivery in the 2027 time frame. North Korea has used both plutonium and highly enriched uranium (HEU) to build nuclear weapons. We address North Korea's efforts to produce these critical nuclear materials and how this production provides us with a means for estimating the actual number of North Korean nuclear weapons. We also address what North Korea's nuclear weapon tests tell us about the explosive power (*yield*) of these weapons. In addition, although there has never been definitive proof of nuclear warheads in Pyongyang's missile payloads, most analysts project (and the evidence strongly suggests) that North Korea produces nuclear warheads for delivery via its ballistic missiles. Evidence shows that the most-likely warheads are HEU. Ballistic missiles in the inventory include Scud B, C, D, and ER; the No Dong; the Musudan; and the Hwasong-12, -14, and -15. All of these missiles are assessed to be capable of carrying a nuclear warhead (depending on its size and weight), and we will address their capabilities as we analyze them in the missile section of this chapter. Finally, we will address the stockpile of nuclear weapons—both North Korea's present stockpile of nuclear weapons and how we expect them to develop, based on disclosed evidence.

North Korea's Nuclear Weapons: Context and Capabilities

It is important to note that North Korea's nuclear weapons program has grown a great deal in terms of numbers of estimated weapons and the capabilities of these weapons. Its conventional capabilities have also advanced, as demonstrated in its October 2020 parade. This growth has been steady since the program was officially identified by the U.S. intelligence community in 1992. Therefore, in this section, we will address both the plutonium programs and the HEU programs in the North Korean inventory. We will also address Pyongyang's nuclear tests and how they have shown an increasing capability since 2006. Finally, we will address the evidence showing how North Korea likely has developed warheads that could be put on ballistic missiles—some that are capable of striking U.S. territory.

North Korea's plutonium nuclear weaponization program truly began when the Soviet Union completed a 5 megawatt-electric (MWE) reactor near Yongbyon (north of Pyongyang) in 1986. The Soviets (as far as we know) did not pass on technology for weaponization of fissile material produced at the reactor, but the North Koreans were apparently able to develop this technology largely on their own.[1] By 1992, it had become obvious to the world that North Korea was processing material to produce nuclear weapons at the facility in Yongbyon. This is what set off the first North Korean nuclear crisis, which ended in 1994 with the signing of the Agreed Framework.[2] Unfortunately, even as the Agreed Framework was being signed, North Korea was entering into a deal with Pakistan that largely involved trading No Dong missiles for the technology to enrich uranium and other assistance.[3] This deal probably started around 1994 and continued until 2002 (many have called this a "nukes for missiles" deal—which it was).[4] In 2002, U.S. Assistant Secretary of State for East Asian and Pacific Affairs James Kelly charged the North Koreans with having an illicit HEU nuclear weaponization program even as the Agreed Framework was in effect. This kicked off the second nuclear crisis, as the North Koreans threw out International Atomic Energy Agency (IAEA) inspectors and restarted operations in their Yongbyon facilities. Thus, the "frozen" program was now "unfrozen," even though work on

---

[1]   See Katherine Malus and Hilary Huaici, "How North Korea Got a Seat at the Nuclear Table," Center for Nuclear Studies, July 13, 2018. However, one very senior North Korean defector has argued that North Korea obtained the services of several dozen former Russian nuclear weapon scientists in the early 1990s.

[2]   For more on the events that led to the Agreed Framework, and the agreement itself, see Jeffrey Lewis, "Revisiting the Agreed Framework," 38 North, May 15, 2015b.

[3]   Natural uranium is only about 0.7 percent uranium-235, the isotope required to initiate a nuclear explosion. The level of uranium-235 must be raised (enriched) to 3 to 5 percent for use in a commercial reactor and to much higher levels for nuclear weapons. See U.S. Nuclear Regulatory Commission, "Uranium Enrichment," webpage, last updated December 2, 2020.

[4]   Samuel Ramani, "The Long History of the Pakistan–North Korea Nexus," The Diplomat, August 30, 2016.

nuclear weapons had never ceased because of Pyongyang's nuclear cooperation with Pakistan throughout the life of the Agreed Framework.[5]

North Korea conducted its first test of a nuclear device in 2006. Results of the test showed its yield to be very small—that is to say, 0.5 to 1 kiloton (KT). Just three years later, in 2009, Pyongyang conducted another nuclear test (underground) that showed a yield of around 4 KT.[6] North Korea's third underground test, in February 2013, likely produced a yield of 6 to 7 KT.[7] Not only was the third test the highest yield up to that point, but, according to numerous press sources, high-ranking Iranian officials were there to watch it.[8] North Korea has been assessed for many years (since at least 2006) to have the designs to build a 500-kg HEU warhead capable of being launched on a missile. The most likely missile candidate for this at the time was the No Dong. The warhead designs came as a result of North Korea's nuclear deal with Pakistan. Pakistan acquired No Dong ballistic missiles from the North Koreans over a period that probably began in the mid-1990s and lasted until sometime in 2002.[9] The Iranians acquired the same HEU technology from Pakistan and the same missiles from North Korea—the likely reason for the Iranians' reported presence at North Korea's nuclear tests in 2009 and 2013.[10]

The North Koreans conducted their fourth nuclear test in January 2016. The test was similar in size to their third underground nuclear test—although the North Koreans claimed it was a test of a "hydrogen weapon." Although no major advances were detected, this test proved that North Korea was continuing to work on its nuclear weapon capabilities.[11] North Korea conducted its fifth nuclear weapon test in September 2016. Sig Hecker, probably the foremost U.S. expert on the North Korean nuclear

---

[5] For more details on how North Korea's violations ended the Agreed Framework, see Charles L. Pritchard, "A Guarantee to Bring Kim into Line," Brookings Institution, October 10, 2003.

[6] For more information about North Korea's first two nuclear tests, see Mark Fitzpatrick, *North Korean Proliferation Challenges: The Role of the European Union*, Stockholm, Sweden: Stockholm International Peace Research Institute, Non-Proliferation Paper No. 18, June 2012.

[7] "N.Korea Resumes Tests for Smaller Missile Warheads," *Chosun Ilbo*, February 26, 2015.

[8] "Iranian Nuke Chief Was in N. Korea for Atomic Test," *Times of Israel*, February 17, 2013.

[9] Bill Gertz, "Report: N. Korea Has Nuclear Warheads for Missiles," *Washington Free Beacon*, May 5, 2014; Jeffrey Lewis, "North Korea's Nuclear Weapons: The Great Miniaturization Debate," 38 North, February 5, 2015a; and Jim Wolf, "N.Korea Closer to Nuclear-Tipped Missile: U.S. Expert," Reuters, December 27, 2011.

[10] Larry A. Niksch, *North Korea's Nuclear Weapons Development and Diplomacy*, Washington, D.C.: Congressional Research Service, RL33590, January 5, 2010.

[11] Nick Hansen, Robert Kelley, and Allison Puccioni, "North Korean Nuclear Programme Advances," *Janes*, March 30, 2016; William Mugford and Jack Liu, "North Korea's Yongbyon Nuclear Facility: New Activity at the Plutonium Production Complex," 38 North, September 8, 2015; "N. Korea Digging New Tunnel at Its Nuke Test Site: Official," Yonhap News Agency, October 30, 2015; "North Korea's Nuclear Programme: How Advanced Is It?" BBC, last updated August 10, 2017; James Pearson, "North Korea Nuclear Blast Shows 'Uncanny Resemblance' to Last Test—Analyst," Reuters, January 8, 2016; and Andrea Shalal, David Brunnstrom, and Jonathan Landay, "North Korea Nuclear Test Did Not Increase Technical Capability: U.S.," Reuters, January 19, 2016.

weapon program and a former director of the Los Alamos National Laboratory, estimated that the yield of that weapon was about 15 to 25 KT,[12] sufficient to cause 450,000 to 630,000 fatalities and serious injuries if detonated on Seoul.[13] It was easily the largest test that the North Koreans had conducted up to that time. Once again, North Korea was showing that it was upgrading the yield of its nuclear weapons.[14]

North Korea conducted what was its biggest nuclear test by far in September 2017. Initial estimates of the seismic magnitude of the test were generally upgraded over time, eventually arriving at an estimated warhead yield of around 250 KT.[15] As a likely indicator that North Korea wanted the world to understand what this test meant, the day before the test, North Korean propaganda distributed photos that showed Kim Jong-un receiving a briefing on a two-stage thermonuclear device. The propaganda photos showed what looked like a Hwasong-14 in the background, as observed by experts. North Korea claimed that this test was of a "thermonuclear device." Such a device would pack a powerful punch if launched on an ICBM aimed at the United States or on a theater missile aimed at Seoul; a weapon of 250 KT detonated on New York City could cause roughly 2.9 million deaths and serious injuries, and such a weapon detonated on Seoul could cause about 3.2 million deaths and serious injuries.[16] The evidence suggests that North Korea's nuclear program will continue to grow, as it has done steadily since 2006 (when the first test took place). Therefore, by 2027, it will be larger and more potent than it is as of this writing, in 2020.

Carrying the Nukes: North Korea's Growing Ballistic Missile Inventory

It is not enough for a state to have nuclear weapons. It also must have the platforms to carry those weapons to the country or countries that it wishes to threaten. As addressed earlier, North Korea has been assessed to have a nuclear weaponization capability since the early 1990s. But one of the biggest issues has always been how the North Koreans

---

[12]   Ralph Vartabedian, "North Korea Has Made a Nuclear Weapon Small Enough to Fit on a Missile. How Worried Should the World Be?" *Los Angeles Times*, August 9, 2017.

[13]   These estimates were derived using the NUKEMAP 2 online computer program; a 15-KT weapon and a 25-KT weapon were "detonated" as an optimal airburst over the default Seoul location in the program. See Alex Wellerstein, NUKEMAP 2.7, tool, last updated 2020.

[14]   Kang Jin-kyu and Kang Chan-su, "North Korea's Fifth Nuclear Test Strongest Yet," *JoongAng Daily*, September 9, 2016; and Foster Klug and Kim Tong-Hyung, "Rhetoric or Real? N. Korea Nuclear Test May Be a Bit of Both," Associated Press, September 10, 2016.

[15]   Frank V. Pabian, Joseph S. Bermudez, Jr., and Jack Liu, "North Korea's Punggye-ri Nuclear Test Site: Satellite Imagery Shows Post-Test Effects and New Activity in Alternate Tunnel Portal Areas," 38 North, September 12, 2017.

[16]   These estimates were derived using the NUKEMAP 2 online computer program; a 250-KT weapon was "detonated" as an optimal airburst over the default locations of these cities in the program. See Wellerstein, 2020.

could target the ROK, Japan, and, of course, the United States with this nuclear capability. Their answer was clearly with ballistic missiles. Therefore, in this section, we will address the capabilities of North Korea's ballistic missile programs.

Although many have noted that North Korea is most likely to target U.S. allies or the United States itself with ballistic missiles if it wants to launch a nuclear strike, there is another method that is feasible, although almost completely unmentioned in scholarly or governmental literature. The North Koreans could put even a primitive nuclear device on an innocent-looking trawler or "rust bucket" cargo ship. They could then sail this ship into, for example, Busan, South Korea; or Tokyo Bay, Japan; or the harbor in Long Beach, California; or Norfolk, Virginia, and detonate the device once inside the port. Such an attack would have the potential to kill tens of thousands of people with a single blow. Although some might think that this does not seem possible, all one has to do is look at how skilled North Korea is at re-flagging ships. The North Koreans re-flag ships dozens, if not hundreds, of times per year as part of Pyongyang's large-scale proliferation operations. This is to proliferate weapons and other illicit products to countries around the world (but particularly the Middle East and Africa) despite sanctions that prohibit this activity.[17] If the North Koreans use the same modus operandi to sneak a ship with a nuclear weapon into an unsuspecting port that they have used many times before when sneaking ships with illicit cargo around the world, it would be (and often has been in the past) next to impossible to track the travels of the vessel, making this a real weapons-of-mass-destruction (WMD) threat that Pyongyang clearly has the capability to use.

North Korea has many types of ballistic missiles and great numbers of them, as shown in Table 3.1. The most-basic missiles that North Korea has are in the Scud series. North Korea (thanks to Egypt) has had Soviet-designed Scuds since the late 1970s.[18] North Korea originally acquired a Scud B, but, since the late 1970s, it has built, tested, deployed, and proliferated Scud C, Scud D, and Scud ER (extended range) missiles. These missiles can strike almost every single part of the ROK landmass.[19] In 1993, the North Koreans conducted successful tests of the *No Dong*, a missile that now has a range of at least 1,500 km and can target Tokyo. This missile has also been built, deployed, and proliferated.[20] In 2004, according to press reports, North Korea fielded the *Musudan* missile (called the *Taepo Dong X* at the time). This missile has a range of

---

[17]   Financial Crimes Enforcement Network, "Advisory on North Korea's Use of the International Financial System," FIN-2017-A007, U.S. Department of the Treasury, November 2, 2017; Jake Hulina, "Nothing If Not Persistent: North Korean Exploitation of Fijian and Cambodian Flags at Sea," *Arms Control Wonk*, blog, August 11, 2020; and Sara Perlangeli, "Flagging Down North Korea on the High Seas," Royal United Services Institute, March 29, 2018.

[18]   Nuclear Threat Initiative, "Module 4: Case Study—North Korea's Scud Story," webpage, undated.

[19]   Theodore A. Posto, "North Korean Ballistic Missiles and US Missile Defense," *Physics & Society*, Vol. 47, No. 2, April 2018.

[20]   Charles Vick, "Nodong," Federation of American Scientists, October 20, 2016.

Table 3.1
North Korean Ballistic Missiles

Western Name	North Korean Name	Fuel (liquid or solid)	Approximate Range (km)[a]	Can It Carry Nuclear Weapons?
KN-02	Hwasong-11	Solid	120–170	No
KN-09	Unknown	Solid	200	No
Scud B	Hwasong-5	Liquid	300	Yes
Scud C	Hwasong-6	Liquid	500	Yes
KN-18 (MaRV)	Unknown	Liquid	450+	Unknown
KN-24	Unknown	Solid	450	Probably no
KN-25	Unknown	Solid	400	Probably no
KN-23	Unknown	Solid	700	Yes
Scud-ER	Hwasong-9	Liquid	1,000	Yes
KN-11	Pukguksong-1	Solid	1,200	Yes
No Dong	Hwasong-7	Liquid	1,500	Yes
KN-15	Pukguksong-2	Solid	1,200–2,000	Yes
KN-26	Pukguksong-3	Solid	1,900	Yes
Musudan	Hwasong-10	Liquid	2,500–4,000	Yes
KN-17	Hwasong-12	Liquid	4,500	Yes
KN-08	Hwasong-13	Liquid	9,000	Yes
KN-14	Unknown	Liquid	6,700	Yes
KN-20	Hwasong-14	Liquid	10,000+	Yes
KN-22	Hwasong-15	Liquid	12,000	Yes
KN-26	Hwasong-15a?	Liquid	13,000?	Yes

SOURCES: Missile Defense Advocacy Alliance, "North Korea," webpage, March 2019; and Missile Defense Project, "Missiles of North Korea," webpage, *Missile Threat*, Center for Strategic and International Studies, last updated November 30, 2020.

NOTES: MaRV = maneuvering reentry vehicle.

[a] The missile range varies with the payload carried.

up to 4,000 km and the potential to hit Guam. It has also been proliferated to Iran.[21] Since 2019, the North Koreans have been test-launching a new missile, designated the *KN-23*, that seems related to the Russian missile known as the *Iskander*. This is a

---

[21]   Daniel Wertz, *North Korea's Ballistic Missile Program*, Washington, D.C.: National Committee on North Korea, December 2017.

solid-fuel ballistic missile with a range of up to 700 km. It is far more accurate than most of North Korea's other ballistic missiles and can potentially carry a nuclear warhead. Unlike the more-primitive Scud missiles, it is able to evade missile defenses.[22] All of these missiles are mobile missiles. In other words, they all come on a TEL, which makes them much more difficult to target. In addition, most are assessed to be capable of carrying a nuclear warhead, as shown in the table.

Although all of the missiles just discussed are dangerous to the security of nations in the region, there are many more. The missile that the North Koreans call the *Hwasong-12* has a range of 4,500 km and has been tested successfully several times. The Hwasong-12 is essentially the first stage of a two-stage missile that the North Koreans call the *Hwasong-14*. This missile has a range of around 6,700 km, enough to hit Anchorage, Alaska. Also using the Hwasong-12 as its first stage is the Hwasong-15, which has a range of up to 12,000 kilometers and is assessed to be (at the very least) easily capable of hitting anywhere on the West Coast of the United States—or farther. In a military parade in October 2020, a more advanced version of the Hwasong-15 was displayed that looks to be longer and to possibly have the capability to carry MIRVs. None of this (including a MIRV capability) is proven to date, but this newer ICBM is bigger and might be an improvement on the Hwasong-15.[23] All of these missiles are also assessed to be capable of carrying a nuclear warhead. All of them are mobile missiles. It is also important to note that several of them are capable of striking U.S. sovereign territory.[24]

The North Koreans also have four other new solid-fuel ballistic missiles. The Poguksong-1 and the Poguksong-3 are submarine-launched ballistic missiles that have the capability to target all of the ROK or Japan. The Poguksong-2 uses the same technology but is a land-launched medium-range ballistic missile. During an October 2020 military parade, a newer missile (untested as of this writing) was displayed that the North Koreans called the *Poguksong-4* and that likely has improvements over the first three versions in this solid-fueled missile series.[25]

Questions have been raised by some scholars about the reentry capability of North Korea's ICBMs. This has been a debate for several years now, although there is little evidence one way or the other. Film of a Hwasong-14 coming down to earth brought an assessment from a well-known analyst in the United States that the missile may have

[22] Geoff Brumfiel, "North Korea's Newest Missile Appears Similar to Advanced Russian Design," NPR, May 8, 2019; and Military-Today.com, "Iskander," webpage, undated.

[23] Choe Sang-Hun, "North Korea Unveils What Appears to Be New ICBM During Military Parade," *New York Times*, last updated January 13, 2021a.

[24] For more assessments on the Hwasong-12, -14, and -15, see Michael Elleman, "The New Hwasong-15 ICBM: A Significant Improvement That May Be Ready as Early as 2018," 38 North, November 30, 2017.

[25] Douglas Barrie and Joseph Dempsey, "What North Korea's Latest Missile Parade Tells Us, and What It Doesn't," International Institute for Strategic Studies, October 12, 2020; and Hyung-jin Kim, "North Korea Says Underwater-Launched Missile Test Succeeded," Associated Press, October 3, 2019.

been breaking up as it was coming to earth. Although this evidence was not definitive, it was highly publicized and raised concern.[26] But other reports have stated that this is not necessarily true and that North Korea likely already has or is close to having reentry capability for its ICBMs.[27] The debate continues. The only way to resolve the debate either way—ever—would be for North Korea to launch an ICBM with a nuclear payload to an empty area of the Pacific Ocean. One hopes that this never happens, but it is certainly a future possibility. Ironically, a newer, bigger, apparently more capable version of the Hwasong-15 was noted in a parade in October 2020. The second stage of this missile looks capable of supporting MIRVs if necessary, although North Korea has never exhibited such a capability. In addition, this missile might have a slightly longer range than the Hwasong-15. Little is known about the missile as of the writing of this chapter.[28] In various ways, North Korea's ICBM capabilities for range, accuracy, and weapon power are likely to be drastically increased by 2027.

Finally, North Korea poses a multifaceted threat to the United States and its allies, to include proliferation. North Korea has sold ballistic missiles capable of carrying nuclear weapons to such countries as Iran, Syria, and Egypt, and even to insurgent groups, such as the Houthis in Yemen.[29] In addition, it now appears that North Korea is proliferating the Hwasong-12 ballistic missile to Iran and the technology for converting it to a two-stage ICBM that is similar to the Hwasong-14 and/or -15.[30]

Stockpiles of Nuclear Material: Plutonium and Highly Enriched Uranium

Predicting the amount of plutonium and HEU produced by North Korea to date is critical to assess nuclear capabilities and threats. Plutonium is produced through reprocessing of spent fuel, and HEU is produced through enrichment. As a baseline, the U.S. intelligence community reportedly indicated that, in mid-2017, North Korea had 30 to 60 nuclear weapons.[31] The lack of strong ROK and U.S. action to deter and counter this magnitude of threat is puzzling. Of further concern, North Korea appears

---

[26] Jesse Johnson, "NHK Video Casts Doubt on North Korean ICBM Re-Entry Capabilities and Effectiveness," *Japan Times*, August 1, 2017.

[27] James Acton, Jeffrey Lewis, and David Wright, "Video Analysis of the Reentry of North Korea's July 28, 2017 Missile Test," Carnegie Endowment for International Peace, November 9, 2018.

[28] Barrie and Dempsey, 2020.

[29] See Bruce E. Bechtol, Jr., *North Korean Military Proliferation in the Middle East and Africa: Enabling Violence and Instability*, Lexington, Ky.: University Press of Kentucky, 2018, pp. 80–137.

[30] Bruce E. Bechtol, Jr., "North Korea, China, and Iran: The Axis of Missiles?" *National Interest*, October 25, 2020.

[31] Albert, 2017.

intent on building more nuclear weapons. According to the National Intelligence Officer for North Korea, Sydney Seiler, "Every engagement in [North Korean] diplomacy has been designed to further the nuclear program, not to find a way out of the nuclear program."[32] Therefore, we project the nuclear weapons threat that North Korea might pose by 2027 as a target for U.S. counters to that threat.

Plutonium

Reactor design specifications, nuclear fuel characteristics, and reactor operation history are required to estimate plutonium production. The nuclear fuel characteristics and reactor design specifications of the 5 MWE Yongbyon Nuclear Reactor are known to some degree through prior nuclear inspections. The duration of reactor operation is calculated through satellite monitoring. Steam from the reactor cooling tower is an indicator that the reactor is in operation. The operation of the reprocessing facility is inferred through the thermal signature of the facility and the activities around the facility, which are monitored by satellite images. Hecker has estimated that the North had 21.3 to 39.6 kg of plutonium inventory as of 2016, with assumptions of some losses of plutonium in reprocessing and fabrication and plutonium consumption for three nuclear tests.[33] Albright has estimated the plutonium inventory to be 23.2 to 37.3 kg as of 2016.[34]

The plutonium inventory has been updated based on the simulated core combustion calculation in a recent report published in Korea. The cumulative amount of nuclear weapons–grade plutonium reprocessed from 2018 to 2019 was estimated to be in the range of 9.12 to 23.65 kg in the report,[35] as broken down in Table 3.2. It was assumed that North Korea reprocessed the entire spent fuel from the 5 MWE reactor during that period. With Hecker's estimation of 21.3 to 39.6 kg through 2016, the total plutonium inventory is estimated to be 30 to 63 kg at the end of 2019. However,

Table 3.2
North Korean Estimated Plutonium Production in 2018 and 2019

Reactor Operation Period	Reprocessing Period	Plutonium Produced
2015–2018	2018	5.3–13.8 kg
2018–2019	2019	3.8–9.9 kg

---

[32] Volodzko, 2021.

[33] Siegfried S. Hecker, Chaim Braun, and Chris Lawrence, "North Korea's Stockpiles of Fissile Material," *Korea Observer*, Vol. 47, No. 4, Winter 2016.

[34] David Albright, "North Korea's Nuclear Capabilities: A Fresh Look," presentation slides, Washington, D.C.: Institute for Science and International Security, April 22, 2017.

[35] Jooho Whang, *Research on Nuclear Threat Crisis Management Countermeasures in Neighboring Countries in Terms of Nuclear Nonproliferation and Nuclear Security*, Seongnam, South Korea: Korea Foundation of Nuclear Safety, July 10, 2019.

this calculation is expected to have great uncertainty because it is based on various assumptions, including operation period, reactor power level, and the efficiency of the reprocessing process. This 2019 reprocessing could add one to two nuclear weapons to the 2017 inventory described earlier.

Highly Enriched Uranium

It is even more difficult to estimate HEU production because of insufficient information on the enrichment facilities. North Korea is using centrifuges to enrich uranium. The inventory and annual production amount of HEU can be estimated based on enrichment capacity, which is mainly dependent on the number and efficiency of centrifuges. However, estimates of HEU production carry uncertainties because enrichment facilities leave only a small amount of physical footprint in construction and operation and are easy to cover up. Moreover, material-related technologies, such as carbon fiber development, might cause a rapid increase in the HEU stockpiles.

North Korea is constantly trying to increase stockpiles of HEU. Estimating HEU stockpiles is considerably more important than estimating plutonium stockpiles to predict North Korea's nuclear capability, because HEU appears to be North Korea's main source for nuclear weapons today.[36] North Korea's scientists disclosed North Korea's uranium enrichment facility to Hecker in November 2010, and they said that the facility consisted of about 2,000 centrifuges at that time.[37] North Korea's scientist explained that the Yongbyon enrichment facility had just been completed and that it was producing 3.5 percent enriched uranium for light water reactors.[38] North Korea also claimed that the facility had a capacity of 8,000 kg-SWU (separative work units) per year.[39] It was estimated that, if the facility was modified to produce HEU, approximately 40 kg of HEU per year could have been produced with 2,000 centrifuges.[40] The enrichment capacity was based on the 2010 observations, with the assumption that the facility was configured to produce HEU. In 2012, Albright estimated North Korea's enrichment capacity to be 4.17 to 17 kg of HEU per 1,000 centrifuges, and the lower bound was the value when assuming high inefficiency in operation of North Korea's centrifuges.[41]

[36]   The North Korean nuclear reactor used to produce plutonium appears to have been shut down for some time. See Josh Smith, "North Korea Nuclear Reactor Site Threatened by Recent Flooding, U.S. Think-Tank Says," Reuters, August 12, 2020.

[37]   Siegfried S. Hecker, *A Return Trip to North Korea's Yongbyon Nuclear Complex*, Nautilus Institute for Security and Sustainability, NAPSNet Special Reports, November 22, 2010.

[38]   Hecker, 2010.

[39]   Hecker, 2010.

[40]   Hecker, Braun, and Lawrence, 2016, p. 735.

[41]   David Albright and Christina Walrond, *North Korea's Estimated Stocks of Plutonium and Weapon-Grade Uranium*, Washington, D.C.: Institute for Science and International Security, August 16, 2012, p. 23.

However, it is exceedingly difficult to find out whether there is a large number of enrichment facilities that are being hidden and whether they are in constant operation. Although North Korea claims that there is no other enrichment facility, Hecker has insisted that there is at least one additional enrichment facility.[42] There are also many signs of expanding the nuclear program in Yongbyon.[43] At the end of 2013, the enrichment facility was expanded an additional 100 m, and it is estimated that the capacity roughly doubled.[44]

Estimates of North Korea's HEU production up through 2016 are shown in Table 3.3. Albright claimed that North Korea's HEU stockpile ranged from 175 to 645 kg at the end of 2016.[45] Hecker's estimate on North Korea's HEU stockpile, which he based on Bistline's calculation, ranges from 300 to 450 kg at the end of 2016.[46] Bistline and colleagues attempted to establish uncertainty in the production of HEU, considering the limitations in the supply of critical materials required for the construction of centrifuges.[47]

Table 3.3
Estimated Highly Enriched Uranium in North Korea's Stockpile

Reference	HEU Stockpile (2016)	Annual Production Rate
Albright	175–645 kg	38–186 kg/year
Hecker (Bistline et al., 2015)	300–450 kg	150 kg/year

---

[42] According to Hecker,

> The Yongbyon centrifuge facility could not have been constructed from scratch and made operational in only 18 months, between April 2009 and November 2010, as Pyongyang has claimed. It is likely that the North had one full cascade (about 340 centrifuges) operational at a separate site long before it moved into the renovated Yongbyon fuel fabrication building and revealed their centrifuge program in November 2010. (Siegfried S. Hecker, *Can the North Korean Nuclear Crisis Be Resolved?* Stanford, Calif.: Center for International Security and Cooperation, Stanford University, March 21, 2012, p. 8)

[43] David Albright and Robert Avagyan, *Recent Doubling of Floor Space at North Korean Gas Centrifuge Plant: Is North Korea Doubling Its Enrichment Capacity at Yongbyon?* Washington, D.C.: Institute for Science and International Security Imagery Brief, August 7, 2013.

[44] Albright and Avagyan, 2013.

[45] Albright, 2017, p. 31.

[46] Hecker, Braun, and Lawrence, 2016.

[47] John E. Bistline, David M. Blum, Chris Rinaldi, Gabriel Shields-Estrada, Siegfried S. Hecker, and M. Elisabeth Paté-Cornell, "A Bayesian Model to Assess the Size of North Korea's Uranium Enrichment Program," *Science & Global Security*, Vol. 23, No. 2, 2015.

Projecting the Nuclear Weapon Inventory

To project the future number of nuclear weapons that North Korea will have,[48] we start by assuming that the 2017 intelligence community estimate of 30 to 60, mentioned earlier, was correct for mid-2017. Plutonium reprocessing would have increased this total to 31 to 62 weapons plus those made via HEU since 2017.[49] We then recognize that there are three possible estimates for the growth rate of the North Korean nuclear weapon inventory. The median estimate is 12 weapons per year, which is based on an article written by Ankit Panda.[50] The high estimate is based on President Trump's comments, made after the 2019 Hanoi Summit, that North Korea had five key nuclear weapon sites.[51] The media have identified four sites as likely North Korean uranium enrichment facilities and have provided an estimate of the number of centrifuges for three of them: 4,000 centrifuges at Yongbyon,[52] 8,000 centrifuges at Kangson,[53] and 10,000 centrifuges at Bungang.[54] There is an unknown number of centrifuges at Sowi-ri.[55] If, as noted earlier, the 2,000 centrifuges at the Yongbyon plant could produce about 40 kg of HEU per year,[56] and the efficiency of the HEU use is up to 80 percent,[57] 22,000 centrifuges could produce about 352 kg of HEU every year. If we

---

[48]   We do not know the number of nuclear weapons that North Korea has assembled from its available critical nuclear material. That part of the nuclear weapon production process is easier for North Korea to hide. For all we know, North Korea could have transformed all of its critical nuclear material into nuclear weapons. For the purposes of this report, we will assume that this is the case, having no source to confirm or deny this to be the case.

[49]   We assume that the 5 MWE reactor at Yongbyon will not likely begin operating again in the future, and that the new reactor at Yongbyon will not contribute plutonium for weapons through 2027. This is clearly a conservative assumption.

[50]   Ankit Panda, "US Intelligence: North Korea May Already Be Annually Accruing Enough Fissile Material for 12 Nuclear Weapons," *The Diplomat,* August 9, 2017.

[51]   Sarah Kim, "Trump Tells Fox About 5 Nuclear Sites in North," *JoongAng Daily*, May 21, 2019.

[52]   Albright and Avagyan, 2013.

[53]   According to the *Washington Post*, "Meanwhile, the North Koreans also have operated a secret underground uranium enrichment site known as Kangson, which was first reported in May by the *Washington Post*. That site is believed by most officials to have twice the enrichment capacity of Yongbyon" (Ellen Nakashima and Joby Warrick, "North Korea Working to Conceal Key Aspects of Its Nuclear Program, U.S. Officials Say," *Washington Post*, June 30, 2018).

[54]   Jeong Yong-Soo, Baek Min-Jeong, and Shim Kyu-Seok, "Secret Enrichment Plant Is Right Next to Yongbyon: Sources," *JoongAng Daily*, March 5, 2019.

[55]   jin0619@donga.com, "NK Has Built Uranium Enrichment Facilities," *Dong-A Ilbo*, February 18, 2009.

[56]   Hecker, Braun, and Lawrence, 2016, p. 735.

[57]   David Albright, *Future Directions in the DPRK's Nuclear Weapons Program: Three Scenarios for 2020*, Washington, D.C.: US-Korea Institute at SAIS, 2015.

assume that each warhead requires 20 kg of HEU,[58] North Korea could add up to 18 nuclear warheads every year.

In Figure 3.1, we estimate North Korea's number of nuclear weapons from 2017 through 2027, with the starting value of 30 to 60 nuclear weapons in 2017, with one to two plutonium weapons added by 2020, and with the numbers growing by either 12 weapons per year (120 total by 2027) or 18 weapons per year (180 total by 2027). These estimates suggest that, in 2020, North Korea already could have had 67 to 116 nuclear weapons, and, by 2027, North Korea might have 151 to 242 nuclear weapons.[59]

Figure 3.1
Projecting the North Korean Nuclear Weapon Inventory

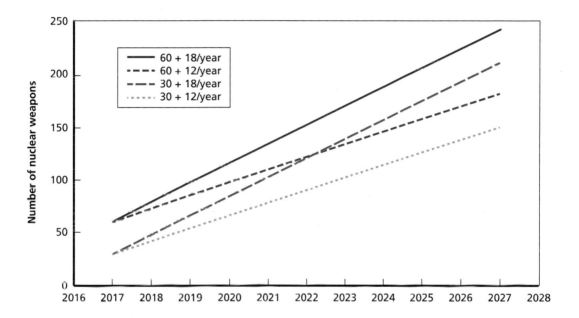

A Caution on Projecting the North Korean Nuclear Weapon Inventory

There are vast uncertainties associated with estimating the number of North Korean nuclear weapons, let alone making any future projections. One key uncertainty is asso-

---

[58] Albright and Walrond, 2012.

[59] To maintain his legitimacy, Kim Jong-un must follow the policies of his father and grandfather. In the 1980s and early 1990s, Kim's grandfather attempted to build two nuclear reactors that could have produced enough fissile material for 50 nuclear weapons per year, or 500 nuclear weapons in a ten-year period. See Federation of American Scientists, "Yongbyon [Nyongbyon] N39°48' E125°48'," webpage, last updated March 4, 2000; and Hecker, Braun, and Lawrence, 2016, p. 729. North Korean uranium enrichment is not supporting quite as rapid a buildup but is reportedly being expanded rather than slowed.

ciated with the fact that these estimates are based on the amount of fissile material that North Korea is believed to have produced, and not on actual nuclear weapon production, about which relatively little is known.[60] A second uncertainty is the actual number of operational centrifuges operating to produce HEU at the identified North Korean facilities, which could be more or fewer than reported. A third uncertainty is whether there are North Korean facilities that are producing fissile material, or that will begin producing fissile material before 2027, that have not been identified and therefore are not included in these projections.

These and other uncertainties should make us cautious in drawing conclusions about the North Korean nuclear weapon threat. However, for the purposes of this chapter, we do know that North Korea has produced nuclear weapons (at least the ones that it has tested, and almost certainly others), is continuing to produce nuclear weapons,[61] and is reportedly increasing its production capacity.[62] The rest of this piece will assume that North Korea might have roughly 200 nuclear weapons by 2027. In the end, it is the intent of the regime and its strategy that concern us; whether the year that North Korea reaches 200 or so nuclear weapons is 2025 or 2030 or even 2040 might not affect our conclusions much other than with regard to how quickly the ROK and the United States need to take action to counter this threat. If North Korea really does have 67 to 116 nuclear weapons in 2020, or even half that many, it already has a large nuclear weapon force that poses a serious threat and against which counters need to be implemented.

---

[60] Some experts recently have begun arguing that North Korea actually has made nuclear weapons with only about one-third of the North's fissile material. The authors have not seen a rationale or source that justifies this percentage.

[61] "No Sign North Korea Reprocessed Plutonium in Past Year, Still Enriching Uranium, IAEA Says," Reuters, September 2, 2020.

[62] Kube, Dilanian, and Lee, 2018.

CHAPTER FOUR

North Korea's Nuclear Weapon Strategy: Trying to Be a Regional Great Power

North Korea's nuclear, missile, and conventional forces are a formidable threat to the United States and its allies in Northeast Asia. Pyongyang's history of provocation and intimidation is a consistent indicator of the regime's intent to achieve its political objectives through the threat or execution of force.

North Korea's nuclear strategy has both driven development of new weapons and, in turn, evolved as new capabilities have been achieved. Pyongyang's continuing development of nuclear and missile programs beyond the necessary requirements for deterrence suggests that the regime strives for a true regional dominance strategy, including warfighting if necessary. Such a development would not only increase the military threat to the region but also raise the potential for greater regime willingness to engage in even more-provocative behavior, as well as coercive diplomacy and more-serious action against the ROK and Japan.

The increasing viability of North Korea's ability to target the continental United States with nuclear weapons has reinforced growing ROK and Japanese fears of abandonment and decoupling of the alliances. They increasingly question whether the United States would be "willing to trade San Francisco for Seoul," raising doubts as to the strength of the U.S. extended deterrence guarantee. Such misgivings could lead Seoul to be more accommodating to Pyongyang and could lead Tokyo to question its own willingness to risk nuclear attack to support allied operations on the Korean Peninsula.

Nuclear Doctrine Evolved as Capabilities Improved

Pyongyang has not disclosed detailed information on its nuclear strategy. However, regime public statements provide insights. In addition, North Korea's ever-growing nuclear and missile capabilities are the means to implement strategy and, as such, reveal regime intentions.

North Korea's nuclear doctrine evolved in the following phases as the regime augmented and improved its nuclear and missile arsenals:

- hiding and denying its nuclear program
- ostensibly portraying the nuclear program as a diplomatic bargaining chip
- deterring U.S. strategic nuclear threat by imposing unacceptable losses with a retaliatory strike
- dissuading and defeating allied invasion with battlefield or tactical nuclear weapons against superior conventional forces
- enabling preemptive nuclear strike against an imminent U.S. counterforce and/ or decapitation strike
- working toward operationalizing a nuclear warfighting capability to undermine the U.S. extended deterrence guarantee and potentially impose unification.

North Korean Doctrinal Statements

As late as January 2003, North Korea still claimed that it had "no intention of developing nuclear weapons. . . . nuclear activities will be limited to . . . generation of electricity."[1] But, five months later, Pyongyang finally publicly acknowledged its nuclear weapons, declaring that, in response to the hostile U.S. policy, the regime would build up a "nuclear deterrent force [that was] not aimed to threaten or blackmail others."[2] This set the tone for years of regime statements that its nuclear weapons were for self-defense, as a deterrent against U.S. nuclear or conventional attack.

In 2012, North Korea revised its constitution to enshrine itself as a nuclear weapon state.[3] Kim Jong-un established the Strategic Rocket Command (later renamed the Strategic Force) as an independent military force equal to the ground, air, navy, and air defense force that reported directly to him and the military General Staff.[4]

In 2013, North Korea codified the role of its nuclear forces during a meeting of the Central Committee of the Korean Workers' Party, where it adopted the Law on Consolidating the Position of Nuclear Weapons State. North Korea characterized its use of nuclear weapons as follows:

> They serve the purpose of deterring and repelling the aggression and attack of the enemy against the DPRK [Democratic People's Republic of Korea] and deal-

---

[1]   Dong-Ki Sung, "North Korea Announces It Has No Intention of Developing Nuke Weapons," *Dong-A Ilbo*, January 22, 2003. However, the Yongbyon nuclear reactor reportedly was not attached to the electrical grid, at least before 2005 (Nicholas Eberstadt, "A Skeptical View," *Wall Street Journal*, September 21, 2005, p. 26).

[2]   Edward Roy, "Bush Administration Unmoved by North Korea's Nuclear Statements," ABC, June 10, 2003.

[3]   "N. Korea Calls Itself 'Nuclear-Armed State' in Revised Constitution," Yonhap News Agency, May 30, 2012; and "N.Korea Puts Nuclear Arms in Constitution," *Chosun Ilbo*, May 31, 2012.

[4]   Choi Ha-young and John G. Grisafi, "North Korea's Nuclear Force Reshuffles Its Politics, Economy," NK News, February 11, 2016.

ing deadly retaliatory blows at the strongholds of aggression until the world is denuclearized. . . .

The DPRK shall take practical steps to bolster up the nuclear deterrence and nuclear retaliatory strike power both in quality and quantity . . . .

The nuclear weapons of the DPRK can be used only by a final order of the Supreme Commander of the Korean People's Army to repel invasion or attack from a hostile nuclear weapons state and make retaliatory strikes. . . .

The DPRK shall neither use nukes against the non-nuclear states nor threaten them with those weapons unless they join a hostile nuclear weapons state in its invasion and attack on the DPRK.[5]

The policy reflected an assured-retaliation strategy of "deterrence by punishment" whereby nuclear weapons would deter allied attacks, including preemptive ones, by threatening a strong nuclear reprisal to inflict unacceptable losses on the United States. There was no distinction made between military and civilian targets.

The regime sought to decouple the U.S. alliances with the ROK and Japan prior to hostilities by emphasizing that its nuclear response would be directed against only the United States, and not the ROK or Japan *unless* they joined the U.S. hostile action.

Implementing the strategy would require only a small nuclear force, but one that could credibly survive an opponent's initial nuclear or conventional strike to retaliate and inflict high casualties or devastation. North Korean efforts to prevent the United States from attacking and destroying its nuclear weapons have focused on denying information about the location of its nuclear weapons. The nuclear arsenal could compensate for North Korea's deteriorating conventional forces.

North Korea's Preemption Threats

As Pyongyang's nuclear and missile prowess increased, so did its threats of a preemptive nuclear attack. Even prior to admitting that North Korea had nuclear weapons, since 1994, North Korean officials had warned, "We will not give you time to collect troops around Korea to attack us. . . . if it is clear you are going to attack, then we will attack."[6]

In 2013, North Korea's Ministry of Foreign Affairs announced that North Korea would "exercise the right to a preemptive nuclear attack to destroy the strongholds of

---

5   "2013 Plenary Meeting of WPK Central Committee and 7th Session of Supreme People's Assembly," 2013.

6   Bureau of Intelligence and Research, "The Secretary's Morning Intelligence Summary," U.S. Department of State, March 29, 1994, p. 11. See also Van Jackson, "Preventing Nuclear War with North Korea: What to Do After the Test," *Foreign Affairs*, September 11, 2016.

the aggressors."[7] In 2016, the ministry declared, "A decisive preemptive attack is the only way for the DPRK to beat back the sudden surprise attack of the U.S. . . . It is a quite natural exercise of the right to self-defense."[8] The National Defense Commission warned that North Korea could conduct a "preemptive and offensive nuclear strike" if it believed that the United States was about to conduct a decapitation strike or military operations to "bring down its social system."[9]

Improving Nuclear Capabilities Enable a New Strategy

Pyongyang's evolving nuclear and missile forces increasingly provide the regime with the ability to conduct a surprise preemptive first strike, a retaliatory second strike, and battlefield counterforce attacks. Pyongyang is producing a new generation of advanced missiles that are more accurate, mobile, and solid-fueled to make them more survivable and difficult to target and that have a greater ability to evade allied missile defenses. The North's solid-fueled missiles also allow quicker launches that are accurate enough to go after hardened or battlefield military targets.

Pyongyang has an extensive and diversified missile force to attack targets in the ROK, Japan, U.S. bases in the Pacific, and the continental United States. The enhanced accuracy of the missiles tested in 2019 and 2020 and their potential ability to defeat allied missile defenses enable North Korea to accomplish effective counter-military attacks against ROK territory with fewer missiles.

As its nuclear arsenal improved, the regime adopted an asymmetric escalation strategy in which Pyongyang could viably threaten a preemptive first strike attack with tactical nuclear weapons to deter or defeat a conventional offensive by superior U.S. and ROK conventional forces.[10] The regime would keep its nuclear ICBMs that threatened the U.S. homeland in reserve to maintain strategic deterrence.

In 2012, Kim directed the preparation of a new war plan for invading the ROK that was designed to neutralize much of the ROK and U.S. conventional force superiority.[11] A major element of this plan was early nuclear weapon use. This plan is discussed in more detail in the section on major warfare with nuclear weapons.

---

[7]   Dashiell Bennett, "North Korea Is Now Threatening a Preemptive Nuclear Attack," *The Atlantic*, March 7, 2013.

[8]   "National Defense Commission, Foreign Ministry Issues Statements on Foal Eagle, Key Resolve," North Korea Leadership Watch, March 6, 2016.

[9]   "National Defense Commission, Foreign Ministry Issues Statements on Foal Eagle, Key Resolve," 2016.

[10]   Vipin Narang, *Nuclear Strategy in the Modern Era, Regional Powers and International Conflict*, Princeton, N.J.: Princeton University Press, 2014, pp. 19–20.

[11]   The North Korean military parade on October 10, 2020, showed examples of substantial North Korean conventional military force modernization. It is unlikely that North Korea has the economic resources to spread these capabilities throughout the North Korean military any time soon. However, the North wants its neighbors and the United States thinking that it has much greater conventional military power than was demonstrated historically.

Evolving Contexts for North Korean Nuclear Weapon Use

North Korea likely envisions several contexts in which it would use, or threaten to use, nuclear weapons. We present five here.

Nuclear Weapons for Intimidation, Coercion, and Deterrence

Until about 2009, North Korea likely could not have delivered a properly function-ing nuclear weapon against a target in the ROK or other countries;[12] therefore, since the Korean War, "the value of the weapons seems to be in the threat of using them, not in their actual use."[13] North Korea has threatened the surrounding countries and the United States for deterrence and many other purposes. Its ability to use nuclear weapons in actual conflict situations, as described in the other contexts, are its most convincing means for deterrence. North Korea also uses its nuclear weapons to cast a "nuclear shadow" over its other provocations—to convince the ROK and the United States to accept North Korean misbehavior and blackmail in peacetime, fearing a potential escalation spiral to nuclear war. For example, North Korea could work with the current ROK government and ROK groups that are favorable to the North to get the ROK to abandon the Northern Limit Line (NLL) imposed by the UNC as the North-South boundary in the West Sea after the Korean War. If North Korean pres-sure failed to achieve this objective, the North could announce that it would no longer accept the NLL, identify its own preferred boundary, and start actively firing artillery as part of exercises across the NLL into waters or even islands that it claims are North Korean territory. Or, the North could use its forces to seize one of the ROK Northwest Islands,[14] using only conventional means but with explicit threats of nuclear weapon use should the ROK attack the captured island. The North might hope that the ROK, fearing escalation, would decide not to respond to the North Korean military actions and would accept the North Korean boundary adjustment or island seizure; this would appear to be a great victory for Kim (and a success that he needs after so many failures). There would be no actual nuclear weapon use unless the ROK or the United States decided to respond militarily, although a nuclear weapon test done before such a cam-paign might heighten the pressure on the ROK government.

By the early 1990s, North Korea likely had sufficient plutonium for one to two nuclear weapons, although they were likely crude devices that it could not yet deliver

---

[12] North Korea's first nuclear test, in 2006, produced a low yield that suggested that the nuclear weapon design was not yet very good. It was not until the second test, in 2009, that the North appeared to be getting to a prop-erly functioning nuclear weapon that may have been mountable on a ballistic missile. See Jeong Yong-soo and Ser Myo-ja, "North Shrank Its Nukes Pre-2014," *Joong-Ang Daily*, August 11, 2017.

[13] Anna Fifield, "North Korea's Making a Lot of Threats These Days. How Worried Should We Be?" *Washing-ton Post*, March 10, 2016b.

[14] North Korea has developed a hovercraft base to support such an attack. See Joseph S. Bermudez, Jr., "New Hovercraft Base at Sasŭlp'o," *KPA Journal*, Vol. 2, No. 2, February 2011.

to a target.[15] As noted in Chapter Two, in 1993, North Korea faced its first nuclear crisis with the United States and worried about losing a potential war with the United States. If the regime were jeopardized in this manner, Kim Jong-il reportedly threatened, he would "destroy the Earth."[16] Kim Jong-il could not really have destroyed the earth, even with nuclear and biological weapons, but he could have created considerable damage. When asked about this story, a senior-elite North Korean refugee said that the regime openly told this story, hoping to deter international action that might cause the regime to collapse, and to intimidate the United States, in particular, to make a favorable nuclear agreement with North Korea.[17]

By executing this kind of ultimate act of defiance, if the North were losing a major war, Kim Jong-un might coerce the ROK and the United States into early war termination and avenge regime destruction if that coercion failed to stop a losing conflict. Because survival is the number-one goal of the North Korean regime, this strategy likely caused the early North Korean nuclear weapons to be planned for targeting ROK, Japanese, and Chinese cities to coerce termination of a conflict, if possible, when the North was on the brink of defeat. If the coercion failed, then the surviving weapons likely would have been fired at these targets to avenge the end of the regime.

In addition, the North has used nuclear weapons for provocations. It has tested its nuclear weapons, seeking to confirm that it had a viable design for them but also to announce to the world that it had achieved the ability to produce them. North Korea did its first test in 2006, and it now has completed a total of six nuclear weapon tests that we know of. Each of the tests put a significant amount of pressure on neighboring countries to negotiate with North Korea for nuclear weapon elimination, although the neighbors knew that elimination would require some compromises on their part. North Korea coerced these compromises without any denuclearization on its part, establishing a pattern of North Korean coercive use of nuclear weapons in peacetime.[18]

Limited Nuclear Weapon Use

Early in its nuclear weapon development, the North likely broadened its nuclear employment strategy and at least its coercive threats to include limited nuclear countervalue attacks for coercive purposes. For example, in 1994, the North Korean representative to South-North talks threatened to turn Seoul into a "Sea of Fire."[19] It is not clear that he was referring to nuclear weapon use, although similar North Korean

---

[15] "North Korean Nuclear Weapons," CIA estimate for Congress, November 19, 2002.

[16] Kim, 2009.

[17] Interview with North Korean senior-elite refugee, Seoul, December 2012.

[18] For North Korea, the downside of its nuclear weapon tests were the UN Security Council Resolutions that followed each nuclear weapon test, applying sanctions on the North.

[19] Minn Chung, "Seoul Will Become a Sea of Fire . . . ," *Bulletin of Concerned Asian Scholars*, Vol. 26, No. 1–2, 1994.

threats since then apparently have referred to nuclear weapon use. For example, Pyongyang vowed to initiate a preemptive two-stage nuclear attack against the ROK leadership, including turning the presidential Blue House into a "sea of fire," if the regime perceived even a "slight sign" of U.S. or ROK preparations for a decapitation strike on the North Korean leadership.[20] As noted in Chapter Three, this kind of attack could kill and seriously injure hundreds of thousands to millions of ROK citizens. Threatening Seoul with nuclear attack could be used by North Korea to get the ROK to surrender to North Korea, to stop a counterforce attack on North Korean nuclear weapon forces, or to stop a counteroffensive attack into North Korea. The North warned that, if the allies persisted in preparing decapitation operations, Pyongyang would initiate nuclear attacks against U.S. bases in the Asia-Pacific region and the U.S. mainland.[21] However, the United States likely would not view such an escalation as a limited nuclear attack.

North Korea also might hold Seoul hostage and target other ROK cities. In 2016, Kim Jong-un oversaw several successful Scud and No Dong mobile missile test launches that simulated preemptive nuclear airburst strikes against ROK ports and airfields to be used by the U.S. military.[22] A photo released by North Korean media showed that the missile range would encompass all of the ROK, including the port of Busan, where U.S. reinforcement forces would land.[23] Such an attack would not only have significant military effects (by disrupting the ability of U.S. forces to deploy to Korea because of nuclear damage to the port of Busan) but also place political pressure on the ROK government to terminate a conflict or to surrender before more ROK cities suffered nuclear attack. In these various cases, if North Korea used a limited nuclear weapon attack, it would retain most of its nuclear weapon force, likely hoping to deter a major U.S. nuclear retaliation.[24]

North Korea also could use limited nuclear attacks to shape a major North Korean conventional attack against the ROK, perhaps one that grew from a series of escalating conventional attacks by both sides. When the ROK conventional forces stopped

---

[20]   Choe Sang-Hun, "N. Korea Threatens to Attack S. Korean Presidential Office, *Dong-A Ilbo*, November 23, 2013b. See also Choe Sang-Hun, "North Korea Threatens to Attack U.S. with 'Lighter and Smaller Nukes,'" *New York Times*, March 5, 2013a.

[21]   "KPA Supreme Command Issues Statement," North Korea Leadership Watch, February 23, 2016.

[22]   Jack Kim, "North Korea Says Missile Test Simulated Attack on South's Airfields," Reuters, July 19, 2016; "Kim Jong Un Observes and Guides Ballistic Missile Drill," North Korea Leadership Watch, July 19, 2016; "Kim Jong Un Observes and Guides Mobile Ballistic Missile Drill and Watches KPA Tank Competition," North Korea Leadership Watch, March 10, 2016; and Shin Hyon-hee, "N.K. Says Missile Test Aimed at Ports, Airfields in the South," *Korea Herald*, July 20, 2016.

[23]   Photo of Kim Jong-Un observing a missile test launch, distributed by Yonhap News Agency, 2016.

[24]   The United States has offered the ROK "extended deterrence" against North Korean nuclear weapon use against the ROK. The U.S. nuclear umbrella promises a U.S. nuclear retaliation against North Korean nuclear weapon use so that the ROK does not need its own nuclear weapons.

the North Korean offensive, the ROK and the United States likely would launch a conventional counteroffensive to push the North Korean forces back to the demilitarized zone and then beyond, into North Korea. North Korea might use a few nuclear weapons to target the lead forces of the counteroffensive advancing on North Korean territory, hoping to stop the counteroffensive before it advanced far into North Korea and claiming that the explosions were only nuclear weapon tests on North Korean territory and do not warrant a U.S. retaliation. The North likely would threaten more nuclear weapon attacks on the ROK and U.S. forces if their advance into the North was not halted. The North also might threaten nuclear attacks on ROK cities if the United States launched a nuclear retaliation. The North might even threaten China with nuclear attacks if China refused to help it defeat the advancing ROK and U.S. forces.

Historical North Korean threats have gone beyond the ROK. North Korea is improving its ability to target Japan with nuclear weapons to prevent the flow of forces and logistics to the peninsula. The North could threaten such attacks to intimidate Tokyo to reject the use of Japanese ports, airfields, and bases for U.S. and UNC operations against North Korea. Kim might also seek to seriously damage those facilities if his intimidation fails. North Korea has threatened "to turn Japan into a 'nuclear sea of flames.'"[25] The North has also warned that Tokyo has not yet come to its senses, and "the four islands of the [Japanese] archipelago should be sunken into the sea by the nuclear bomb . . . . Japan is no longer needed to exist near us."[26] North Korea also identified the Japanese cities of Tokyo, Osaka, Yokohama, Nagoya, and Kyoto as targets,[27] to intimidate Tokyo to reject the use of Japanese ports, airfields, and bases for U.S. and UNC operations against North Korea, thereby seriously disrupting the flow of U.S. forces to the ROK. In 2017, Kim observed a missile firing exercise practicing the war plan "to strike the bases of the US imperialist aggressor forces in Japan."[28] The statement was accompanied by a map showing that the missiles were fired to the range of the U.S. Marine Corps Air Station at Iwakuni. In addition, if China were to prepare to intervene in a conflict, North Korea likely would threaten nuclear attacks on Beijing or other Chinese cities to coerce China to abort its preparations for seizing North Korean territory.[29]

---

[25] "N. Korea Threatens to Turn Japan into 'Nuclear Sea of Flames,'" Yonhap News Agency, September 29, 2004.

[26] Andy Sharp, "North Korea Threatens to Use Nuclear Weapon to 'Sink' Japan," NDTV, last updated September 14, 2017. Note that this threat is a bluster because North Korea lacks the nuclear forces to carry it out.

[27] Ministry of Defense of Japan, "Korean Peninsula," in *Defense of Japan 2014*, Tokyo, Japan, 2014, p. 16.

[28] "Kim Jong Un Supervises Missile Drill," North Korea Leadership Watch, March 6, 2017.

[29] According to one source,

> Beijing also appears to be enhancing its capability to seize North Korean nuclear sites and occupy a swath of the country's northern territory. . . . That, they say, would require a much larger Chinese operation than just sealing the border, with special forces and airborne troops likely entering first to secure nuclear sites, followed

North Korea also could use theater nuclear strikes against the U.S. bases in Guam. The Supreme Command of the Korean People's Army warned, "The U.S. should not forget that Anderson Air Force Base in Guam [and] naval bases in Japan and Okinawa . . . are within the striking range of the DPRK's precision strike means."[30] The North Korean Ministry of Foreign Affairs declared that "all the U.S. military bases in the operational theatre in the pacific including Guam will face ruin in the face of all-out and substantial attack."[31] To illustrate its threat, in 2017, Pyongyang announced that it was "carefully examining the operational plan for making an enveloping fire at the areas around Guam with medium-to-long-range strategic ballistic rocket Hwasong-12 in order to contain the U.S. major military bases on Guam including the Anderson Air Force Base."[32] The plan was to have the missiles impact 30 to 40 km on either side of Guam.[33] Foreign Minister Ri Yong-ho subsequently declared that North Korea might conduct a nuclear airburst test of a hydrogen bomb over the Pacific.[34]

If North Korea decides to risk U.S. retaliation by limited use of nuclear weapons, North Korea also could include other types of attack. For example, North Korea might use cyberattacks to complicate an ROK and U.S. response or to create other crises that would split ROK and U.S. attention. It might try to make its use of nuclear weapons plausibly deniable, such as by delivering a nuclear weapon on a foreign merchant ship going to the port of Busan. North Korea learned in 2010, in sinking the ROK warship Cheonan with a torpedo, that it could get many of the internal benefits that it wanted even if it did not openly claim credit for an attack, and could thereby significantly reduce the possibility of a retaliation.

Many U.S. authors discount all of these potential limited nuclear attacks, arguing that North Korea has threatened such attacks for coercive purposes only and that it would never risk a U.S. nuclear retaliation. However, in 1997, the most senior North Korean military defector at the time testified to the U.S. Congress with a different perspective:

> Some Americans believe that even if North Korea possessed the ability to strike the United States, it would never dare to because of the devastating consequences. But

---

by armored ground forces with air cover, pushing deep into North Korea. (Jeremy Page, "China Prepares for a Crisis Along North Korea Border," *Wall Street Journal*, July 24, 2017)

[30] "N. Korea Warns of 'Precision Strike' on U.S. Bases," CBS News, April 5, 2013.

[31] Clynt Ridgell, "North Korea Threatened Guam Numerous Times in the Past," Pacific News Center, August 9, 2017.

[32] Christine Kim and Soyoung Kim, "North Korea Says Seriously Considering Plan to Strike Guam: KCNA," Yahoo News, August 8, 2017.

[33] Jung In-hwan, "Is N. Korea Raising Peninsula Tensions in Bid for US Negotiations?" *Hankyoreh*, August 11, 2017.

[34] "North Korea Ramps Up Threat to Test Hydrogen Bomb over Pacific," *The Guardian*, October 25, 2017.

I do not agree with this idea. . . . Kim Jong-il believes that if North Korea creates more than 20,000 American casualties in the region, the U.S. will roll back and the North Korea will win the war.[35]

Within the past few years, a more senior and more well-placed North Korean military escapee made similar comments, arguing that the North Korean leaders have come to believe that the United States no longer has the stomach for wars with sizable attrition.[36] North Korea may believe that an early, limited nuclear weapon use that instantaneously caused thousands of U.S. casualties would induce U.S. force withdrawal from the ROK.[37] Today, this level of U.S. casualties could be achieved by North Korea detonating a nuclear weapon on the U.S. military headquarters at Camp Humphreys, which North Korea has designated as "our military's foremost strike target."[38] Other U.S. facilities in the ROK also could be targeted, such as the U.S. Army base in Daegu; the U.S. Air Force bases in Osan and Kunsan; and the U.S. pier at the port of Busan, which would be used for disembarking U.S. forces deployed to the ROK.[39] This North Korean view appears to us to be a clear mistake that is likely to lead to the destruction of the North Korean regime, as described in Chapter Five.[40]

---

[35] "North Korean Missile Proliferation," hearing before the U.S. Senate Committee on Governmental Affairs Subcommittee on International Security, Proliferation, and Federal Services October 21, 1997, Washington, D.C.: U.S. Government Printing Office, 1997, p. 5. As bizarre as this perspective sounds to most Americans, Osama bin Laden had a similar perspective, quoted in a 2014 article:

> Turning to the Clinton Administration's withdrawal of U.S. forces from Somalia in 1993 and 1994, Bin Laden was even more scathing. 'Tens of your soldiers were killed in minor battles and one American Pilot was dragged in the streets of Mogadishu you left the area carrying disappointment, humiliation, defeat and your dead with you. Clinton appeared in front of the whole world threatening and promising revenge, but these threats were merely a preparation for withdrawal.' (David Samuels, "How Osama Bin Laden Outsmarted the U.S. and Got What He Wanted," *Tablet*, January 22, 2014)

[36] Interview with North Korean senior military escapee, Seoul, March 2017. The escapee used the example of the 1983 terrorist bombing of the U.S. Marine Corps barracks in Lebanon that led to the subsequent U.S. withdrawal from Lebanon.

[37] North Korea might believe that such an attack would lead to U.S. disengagement, but, if so, this would be a fatal mistake. As the Japanese attack on Pearl Harbor demonstrated, it seems more likely that any adversary that kills thousands of Americans will face the wrath of a united, furious U.S. nation. Although it is impossible to predict with certainty how a U.S. President would react, a President that failed to devastate such an adversary would very likely face impeachment.

[38] Park Won Gon, *Strategic Implications of the USFK Relocation to Pyeongtaek*, Seoul, South Korea: Korea Institute for Defense Analyses, No. 164, October 20, 2017, p. 4.

[39] Mount, 2019.

[40] The kind of North Korean attack postulated in this section seems far more likely to draw a U.S. response akin to the response to the attack on Pearl Harbor than to the response to the attack on the Beirut Marine Corps barracks.

Major Warfare with Nuclear Weapons

The ROK and the United States certainly do not want to fight a major war with North Korea, fearing the extensive destruction and loss of life that would occur. For decades, they have avoided any escalation of the many North Korean provocations that might spiral in that direction. It is probably also the case that North Korea does not want a major war with the ROK and the United States, because such a war would pose serious risks to the survival of the regime. Still, it is unclear that the ROK and U.S. deterrence threat would work if the regime felt serious internal threats and sought a diversionary war against the ROK and the United States.[41] Both sides prepare war plans for major war as a way of training their military forces, deterring offensive action by the other side, and being ready to effectively fight if deterrence fails. Both sides apply security measures to conceal the details of their war plans from each other.

Because of these security measures, the ROK and the United States do not know a great deal about the North Korean plans. Nevertheless, the evidence suggests that North Korea primarily plans for invasion of the ROK to impose Korean unification, aligning its war plans with its national objectives. Although North Korean conventional military forces are numerically superior to ROK and U.S. conventional forces deployed in the ROK, Kim surveyed his conventional forces soon after establishing himself as the leader of North Korea in 2012 and concluded that conventional conflict with the ROK and the United States would almost certainly end badly for North Korea, and the regime in particular.[42] So, he directed the North Korean military to develop a new strategy to invade and occupy Seoul within three days and all of the ROK within seven days. North Korea had studied U.S. operations in Afghanistan and Iraq and concluded that it must prevail quickly, before U.S. reinforcements could arrive. Accomplishing these objectives would necessitate significant early use of nuclear weapons and other asymmetric capabilities.[43] The phases of this plan are as follows:

> ... the first phase is surprise attacks with nuclear missiles; the second phase is total war; the third phase is total attacks with asymmetric combat power; the fourth phase is special operations in the rear; and the final step is conquering the whole Peninsula. Based on this plan, North Korea's nuclear strategy has been developed as a core asset for waging a unification war.[44]

North Korea might hope that, with integrated actions to disrupt ROK and U.S. missile defenses, a North Korean surprise attack of 40 to 60 nuclear weapons against

---

[41]   See, for example, Jack S. Levy, "The Diversionary Theory of War: A Critique," in Manus I. Midlarsky, ed., *Handbook of War Studies*, Boston, Mass.: Unwin Hyman, 1989.

[42]   Thae, 2020.

[43]   Jeong and Ser, 2015. This strategy appears to be the only logical alternative for Kim, as long as he can prevent serious U.S. nuclear retaliation. After all, a leader does not train his military forces to lose.

[44]   Chung, 2016, p. 468.

military and political targets in the ROK could disable a significant amount of ROK and U.S. air and naval force capabilities and command and control,[45] giving the North a substantial margin of superiority for an invasion of the ROK and perhaps even the ability to dictate ROK surrender. The North also might hope to disable the ROK and U.S. military forces with cyber, electronic warfare, and special operations forces attacks on ROK and U.S. command, control, communications, and intelligence in an attempt to blind, disable, delay, or misdirect ROK and U.S. responses, presumably starting these efforts even before the formal military attack. North Korean conventional and chemical artillery fire along the demilitarized zone and deeper likely would contribute to a favorable outcome for the North.

If the ROK and the United States were to launch a counteroffensive into North Korea, the North has threatened a preemptive attack:

> [The attack would] burn up all the objects in the areas under the control of the first and third field armies . . . including Seoul . . . and will lead to the all-out attack for neutralizing the launch bases of the U.S. . . . forces in the Pacific operational theatre together with the simultaneous strike at the depth of the whole of the southern half [of the peninsula].[46]

North Korea has also warned that "any military conflict on the Korean Peninsula is bound to lead to an all-out war, a nuclear war . . . the DPRK will blow up the U.S. bases for aggression in its mainland and in the Pacific . . . ."[47] It is easier to understand North Korea's interest in 200 or more nuclear weapons when contemplating this extent of nuclear targeting.

Decoupling U.S. Extended Deterrence for the ROK

Some of the North Korean thinking toward decoupling the ROK-U.S. alliance, described earlier, focuses on limited nuclear attacks to cause a level of U.S. casualties in Korea that would be unacceptable to the United States. North Korea appears to be taking this concept a step further in its development of ICBMs that would be used to

---

[45]   Theater missiles are fired from mobile TELs. The KN-23 likely would be the preferred missile for this kind of attack. Each KN-23 TEL fires two missiles. So, the North would need 20 to 30 KN-23 TELs to execute a near-simultaneous attack.

[46]   Stephen Haggard, "Nuclear Doctrine: What the North Koreans Are Actually Saying," Peterson Institute for International Economics, August 16, 2017. The first and third field armies are the major ROK commands on the demilitarized zone. The ROK and the United States are unlikely to launch a counterattack until North Korean WMD have been sufficiently destroyed to prevent this kind of North Korean attack.

[47]   Max Fisher, "Here's North Korea's Official Declaration of 'War,'" *Washington Post*, March 29, 2013; and pbr@yna.co.kr, "N. Korea Threatens Ultra-Harsh Action on U.S. Soil over Hacking Allegation," Yonhap News Agency, December 21, 2014.

threaten the U.S. homeland with nuclear weapon attack.[48] The North Korean regime might believe that, when it has enough nuclear weapons and ICBMs (maybe 30 to 50),[49] it will be prepared to launch many rounds of ICBM attacks on the United States. For Kim, this can be conceived of as a kind of "game of chicken," in which each side escalates in ways that cause more damage to the other. Kim might hope that the risk-averse United States, fearful of further damage to the U.S. homeland, would stop escalating after one or two rounds.[50] The risks to North Korea that are associated with such a "game of chicken" would be immense; the North would be unlikely to attempt such a thing except in circumstances in which the regime feels internal jeopardy. But Kim also might hope that his eventual ability to launch nuclear attacks against the United States would deter the United States from ever exercising the U.S. nuclear umbrella to retaliate against a North Korean nuclear attack on the ROK, without Kim having to fire a shot.

North Korea's ability to target U.S. cities with thermonuclear weapons could inhibit U.S. execution of its nuclear umbrella and thereby exacerbate growing allied concerns about the viability of the U.S. extended deterrence guarantees. The ROK and Japan have already questioned the willingness of the United States to risk its cities for theirs, much as former French President Charles DeGaulle reportedly believed that France required its own nuclear weapons because the United States would not be prepared to trade New York for Paris.[51] The apparent demise of the U.S. nuclear umbrella could decouple the ROK-U.S. alliance and U.S. domination of the peninsula—a key North Korean objective.

North Korean ICBMs also would give North Korea the opportunity to retaliate directly against the United States if the United States mounted a counterforce

---

[48] Pyongyang has threatened to "reduce the US mainland to ashes and darkness" (Bryan Harris, "North Korea Threatens Nuclear Destruction of Japan," *Financial Times*, September 14, 2017). In 2013, Kim was photographed in front of a map labeled "U.S. Mainland Strike Plan," with missile trajectories aimed at Washington, D.C.; U.S. Indo-Pacific Command in Hawaii; San Diego, California (a principal homeport of the Pacific Fleet); and Barksdale Air Force Base in Louisiana (home of Air Force Global Strike Command) (Jeffrey Lewis, "North Korean Targeting," *Arms Control Wonk*, blog, April 8, 2013).

[49] The defense of the continental United States is currently provided by 44 Ground-Based Interceptors in Alaska and California. Several interceptors likely would be fired at each incoming North Korean missile because the current North Korean ICBM arsenal is small, and some number of North Korean ICBMs would still likely leak through this defense. Once North Korea deploys 30 to 50 ICBMs, it probably would have enough to exhaust the U.S. defenses and then deliver some ICBMs against the United States without opposition.

[50] In the words of one source, "Which is better prepared for nuclear exchange, North Korea or the USA? . . . For their part, the North Koreans are highly motivated candidate martyrs well prepared to run the risk of having the whole country exploding in nuclear attacks from the USA by annihilating a target population center" (Kim Myong Chol, "Farewell to 1994 Agreed Framework!" Northeast Asia Peace and Security Network Policy Forum Online, November 24, 1998).

[51] See this story in Bruno Tertrais, "Destruction Assurée: The Origins and Development of French Nuclear Strategy, 1945-81," in Henry D. Sokolski, ed., *Getting MAD: Nuclear Mutual Assured Destruction, Its Origins and Practice*, Strategic Studies Institute, U.S. Army War College, 2004, p. 58.

attack to destroy the North Korean nuclear forces and failed to destroy some of the North Korean forces. Would a U.S. President take the risk of numerous U.S. cities being attacked by hydrogen bombs?[52] North Korea probably perceives that Washington would be hesitant to preempt North Korean actions.

Nuclear Weapon Proliferation

As the number of North Korean nuclear weapons hits 100 or so, the North Korean leaders might perceive that they could make some of those weapons available for sale. This would be especially true if North Korea continues to be subject to significant UN and U.S. sanctions, depleting its reserves of hard currency.

In his 2019 New Year's address, Kim claimed that the North would not proliferate nuclear weapons: "Accordingly, we declared at home and abroad that we would neither make and test nuclear weapons any longer nor use and proliferate them . . . ."[53] However, because Kim has violated his promise not to make any more nuclear weapons, his promise not to proliferate is subject to substantial doubt.

Overall Perspective

If Kim can develop sufficient nuclear weapon power to accomplish his objectives in these five contexts, he will have made North Korea a powerful country, as called for in the modification of the North Korean constitution, discussed earlier. This position of power is attractive to the North Korean regime given that North Korea is otherwise, in many ways, an impoverished third-world country, not at all the great power that the regime claims. To become a great power, North Korea must have a powerful economy, which can happen only if the UN- and U.S.-imposed sanctions are terminated. Kim has told his leaders that if the North becomes a "nuclear weapon state," its economic problems will be solved.[54] Thus, the North Korean interest in nuclear weapons goes beyond military issues.

But North Korea appears to be seeking more. North Korea wants to be free to impose unification on the ROK in one of the alternative ways that we have described. Kim might believe that the ROK-U.S. alliance can be broken, in significant part by North Korean actions, leading to the withdrawal of U.S. troops from the ROK and termination of the U.S. nuclear umbrella. But this strategy might not work. Kim might not have considered how any ROK government facing a termination of the ROK-U.S. alliance could execute a crash nuclear weapon development program yielding more

---

[52] The fictional nuclear strategist Dr. Strangelove opined, "Deterrence is the art of producing in the mind of the enemy, the fear to attack" (*Dr. Strangelove*, dir. Stanley Kubrick, Columbia Pictures, 1964). North Korea appears to be attempting to create such a fear.

[53] Kim Jong-un, "New Year Address of Supreme Leader Kim Jong Un for 2019," trans. *Rodong Sinmun*, National Committee on North Korea, January 1, 2019.

[54] Choi Hyun-jung, "Kim Jong-il 'Acquired the Status of Nuclear Power in 2012,'" *Dong-A Ilbo*, May 11, 2009.

than a few nuclear weapons, potentially before all U.S. forces were withdrawn from the ROK. If the alliance is broken at some future time, the North would want to act promptly to exercise its nuclear weapons to coerce or militarily impose unification before the ROK would be able to match the North Korean nuclear weapon forces.

North Korea also knows that China aspires to become the global hegemon by 2049.[55] China has dominated the Koreas for centuries and will undoubtedly seek greater domination in the future. Kim might perceive that nuclear weapons can give him the ability to withstand both U.S. and Chinese dominance. A North Korean training lecture describes the regime's apparent objectives:

> The dear supreme commander will dominate the world with the nuclear weapons, will make the U.S. apologize and compensate for us for decades of bullying our people, and will declare to the entire world that the world's powerful order will be reshaped by the Juche-Korea, not the United States.[56]

We do not know whether this is just North Korean wishful thinking or whether it reflects Kim's actual aspirations. Kim clearly does believe that nuclear weapons empower him against adversaries both within and outside North Korea. That thinking will make dismantling the North Korean nuclear weapon program extraordinarily difficult.

Summarizing Potential North Korean Nuclear Weapon Employment

North Korea has not fielded an open description of its nuclear weapon employment strategy. But much can be made about nuclear weapon targeting threats that North Korea has made for decades. As noted in Chapter One, North Korea was talking about counter-military and countervalue nuclear targeting in the 1970s and has since continued the practice. Many of North Korea's statements about how it might use its nuclear weapons likely reflect efforts to coerce and deter other countries and might also reflect how the North would employ its weapons. North Korea has spoken most about nuclear weapon employment to preempt regime defeat, whether that defeat would potentially come because of external attacks or because of failed North Korean aggression.

Much can be made from some of the points of the 2013 Law on Consolidating the Position of Nuclear Weapons State:

---

[55] Brands, 2020.

[56] Baik Sung-won, "Leaked N. Korean Document Shows Internal Policy Against Denuclearization," Voice of America, June 17, 2019a.

1. The nuclear weapons of the DPRK are just means for defence as it was compelled to have access to them to cope with the ever-escalating hostile policy of the U.S. and nuclear threat.

2. They serve the purpose of deterring and repelling the aggression and attack of the enemy against the DPRK and dealing deadly retaliatory blows at the strongholds of aggression until the world is denuclearized.

3. The DPRK shall take practical steps to bolster up the nuclear deterrence and nuclear retaliatory strike power both in quality and quantity to cope with the gravity of the escalating danger of the hostile forces' aggression and attack.[57]

North Korea also regularly speaks of using its nuclear weapons preemptively.[58] North Korea has referred to a series of potential nuclear targets for both operational and strategic purposes in the United States and U.S. territories, the ROK, and Japan.[59] In addition, although North Korea has not spoken about targeting China with nuclear weapons, China has threatened North Korea with attack, as discussed in Chapter Five, and North Korea would almost certainly retaliate against Chinese attacks or threats thereof, much like it would retaliate against the United States.

With this material as background, Table 4.1 is a notional estimate of the number of nuclear weapons that North Korea might allocate for different kinds of use against different countries,[60] depending on the number of nuclear weapons it possesses at any given time. These allocations are important because they give us insights into the total number of nuclear weapons that Kim likely feels that he needs. In the table, strategic employment correlates to North Korean efforts to deter, coerce, and exact revenge against neighboring powers and would be heavily focused on countervalue targets. Operational employment would be associated with warfighting applications and focused on military-related targets. Thus, with 50 nuclear weapons, North Korea might want about 25 for use against command and control facilities, airfields, and ports in the ROK; many of these weapons probably would be for use at the beginning of the conflict, per the seven-day plan described earlier.

---

[57] "Law on Consolidating Position of Nuclear Weapons State Adopted," KCNA Watch, January 4, 2013.

[58] See, for example, Bill Neely, "North Korea Warns It Would Use Nuclear Weapons First If Threatened," NBC News, October 16, 2016.

[59] Léonie Allard, Mathieu Duchâtel, and François Godement, "Pre-Empting Defeat: In Search of North Korea's Nuclear Doctrine," London, United Kingdom: European Council on Foreign Relations, ECFR/237, 2017.

[60] The "Other" strategic category in the table would include Russia, Australia, and countries in Europe.

Table 4.1
Notional North Korean Nuclear Weapon Allocations

Type of Employment and Country Targeted	Number of North Korean Nuclear Weapons		
	50 Total	100 Total	200 Total
Strategic employment			
ROK	5	6	8
Japan	5	8	12
United States	5	12	24
China	5	10	20
Other	0	4	8
Proliferation	0	2	12
Operational employment			
ROK	25	44	78
Japan	2	7	16
United States	0	0	4
China	3	7	18

There are perhaps 20 major Combined Forces Command (CFC)[61] military facilities in the ROK,[62] and there are some more elsewhere. Table 4.1 clearly suggests that, in a major war, North Korea would have difficulty achieving the effects that it would like to achieve using 25 weapons for operational employment out of a total of 50 nuclear weapons. This is because North Korean ballistic missiles have questionable reliability, probably no greater than 70 percent, and many likely targets would be covered by missile defenses. So, even an attack of 25 or so nuclear weapons at the start of a conflict might damage as few as five to ten of these 20 major command and control bases, air force bases, and key ports in the ROK. However, with 100 to 200 total nuclear weapons and serious attempts to suppress or avoid missile defenses (e.g., with the Iskander-like missiles that North Korea tested in 2019 and 2020), an initial North Korean nuclear attack might cause significant damage to the key CFC military facilities, resulting in serious consequences to the ROK and U.S. ability to successfully fight in a conflict.

---

[61]   CFC is the combined ROK-U.S. command for deterring North Korea and defeating it if deterrence fails.

[62]   The ROK has roughly a dozen major military airfields, several major command and control facilities, and perhaps five or so major military-related seaports.

Catalysts for Initiating Nuclear Weapon Use

The use of nuclear weapons appears increasingly likely in any conflict on the Korean Peninsula. That use could be limited to threats and coercion, an application of the so-called nuclear shadow.[63] Or, the use of nuclear weapons could involve the actual launch of nuclear weapons. A key factor in nuclear weapon use would be how a war might start.

Pyongyang might assume that conditions for small-scale military action were favorable and use nuclear threats to coerce Seoul to accept regime demands and deter the United States from responding.

North Korea also could begin with a massive attack, as it did in June 1950, which would be consistent with the seven-day plan. In this context, Pyongyang would begin with a massive artillery, missile, nuclear weapon, and conventional force attack. The regime likely would use chemical weapons—both persistent agents against rear areas to degrade resupply, reinforcement, and attack operations and nonpersistent agents against frontline units to facilitate breakthrough attacks. The regime also might use biological weapons against key ROK and U.S. command and control, airfield, port, and logistical facilities.

Alternatively, the United States could precipitate hostilities by conducting a preemptive or preventive attack on North Korea, as it considered doing in 1994 and 2017. This kind of campaign could be limited to standoff attacks or could involve a full invasion of the North. Such action could trigger a nuclear response either immediately or after allied forces had entered North Korea. Pyongyang also might assess that such an attack was imminent and preempt this preemption.

There is also the potential for stumbling into a major war. A North Korean provocation or tactical-level clash along the border could inadvertently escalate into major strategic conflict. Pyongyang frequently depicts allied military exercises as precursors to an attack on or an invasion of North Korea.

It is uncertain whether the regime's declarations are merely for propaganda purposes or truly reflect a perception that the regime is in imminent danger. Given its poor intelligence and reconnaissance capabilities, the regime could also misperceive allied military exercises or signaling actions as a prelude to attack and decide to preempt what it perceives to be an ROK and U.S. preemption.

Each side could misinterpret the other's intentions, fueling tensions, intensifying a perceived need to escalate, and raising the risk of miscalculation, especially with a

---

[63] In a limited conventional conflict between North Korea and the ROK and the United States, the North Korean nuclear weapons would cast a nuclear shadow that facilitates North Korean attacks by convincing the ROK and the United States not to risk escalated retaliation that could spiral into North Korean nuclear weapon use. This phenomenon is associated with the stability-instability paradox. See Michael Krepon and Chris Gagne, eds., *The Stability-Instability Paradox: Nuclear Weapons and Brinkmanship in South Asia*, Washington, D.C.: Stimson, No. 38, June 2001.

preemptive attack. If the U.S. were to initiate a limited attack on a few targets, would North Korea instead perceive it as the first phase of a major attack and invasion? Pyongyang could assume the worst and rush to use its nuclear weapons out of fear of losing them to the allied preemption in the early stages of hostilities.

The ROK has developed independent preemptive attack plans and acquired weapons that are capable of attacking North Korean WMD.[64] Seoul created a three-part strategy consisting of the kill chain detection and preemptive attack system to target North Korean missiles prior to launch; the Korea Air and Missile Defense System; and the Korea Massive Punishment and Retaliation to attack nuclear, missile, and leadership targets after attack or upon detection of signs of imminent North Korean attack. The ROK defense minister announced that a special forces unit could be used to assassinate the North Korean leadership.[65]

The ROK and the United States might be increasingly forced to rely on a preemption strategy because North Korea's growing nuclear capabilities are an existential threat to the ROK and a potentially serious threat to the United States.

Advocacy of preemption both by North Korea and by U.S allies is destabilizing and could lead to greater potential for either side to miscalculate. Pyongyang might not realize that the more it achieves, demonstrates, and threatens to use its nuclear prowess, the more likely an ROK or U.S. preemption during a crisis becomes.

Conclusion

North Korea has pursued nuclear weapons under the assumption that they are a major source of regime power and survivability. North Korean nuclear weapons certainly could give the regime significant coercive powers and make possible a variety of conflict situations that would be devastating to the peninsula and its neighbors. What North Korea does not seem to recognize is that its nuclear weapons also impose on it serious risks. Although some experts have postulated that nuclear proliferation to such countries as North Korea would tend to stabilize the region,[66] the aggressiveness of Kim might have the opposite effect, especially if Kim fears internal instability. The ROK and the United States have good reasons for seeking the dismantlement of the North Korean nuclear weapon program.

---

[64] Anna Fifield, "In Drills, U.S., South Korea Practice Striking North's Nuclear Plants, Leaders," *Washington Post*, March 7, 2016a.

[65] Andrei Akulov, "South Korea Forms Special Unit to Kill North Korean Leader," Strategic Culture Foundation, January 18, 2017.

[66] Kenneth Waltz, *The Spread of Nuclear Weapons: More May Better*, London, United Kingdom: International Institute for Strategic Studies, *Adelphi Papers*, No. 171, 1981.

CHAPTER FIVE

ROK and U.S. Strategies for Responding to the North Korean Nuclear Weapon Threat

The previous three chapters discuss North Korea's objectives, its nuclear weapon threat, and how it might use its nuclear weapons. This chapter addresses how to respond to North Korean nuclear weapons, concluding that the ROK and the United States must be able to defend themselves against North Korean nuclear weapon use and to defeat North Korea if it uses nuclear weapons. Such abilities will strengthen deterrence and might make North Korea willing to pursue some degree of denuclearization. We also propose other needed actions, including a revised negotiation approach and ideas for how to work with China on this issue.

Key Findings That Drive an ROK and U.S. Counter–Nuclear Weapon Strategy

Chapters One through Four lead us to several findings that should drive U.S. responses to the developing North Korean nuclear weapon threat:

- The principal objectives of the North Korean regime (from Chapter Two) are
  - ensure regime survival and maintain absolute control over North Korea
  - achieve peninsula dominance—i.e., Korean unification of some form under regime control
  - become a regional great power that is able to achieve the first two objectives and to thwart even domination by the United States and China.

- North Korea appears to be trying to field a large nuclear weapon force (perhaps 200 nuclear weapons), potentially by 2027.[1] It also plans growth in its ballistic missile delivery means for nuclear weapons, with especially significant growth in the number of ICBMs that could deliver nuclear weapons to the United States.

---

[1] Note that, if North Korea does not amass 200 nuclear weapons until 2030 or even 2040, the ROK and the United States would still need to deal with much the same threat.

- This number of nuclear weapons would facilitate diverse North Korean threats, outlined in Chapter Four, that could significantly impair ROK and U.S. objectives and security:
  - North Korea could try to use nuclear weapon attacks at the start of a major war with the ROK to neutralize much of the ROK and U.S. air forces deployed in the ROK and major seaports and command and control facilities. Such attacks could leave the ROK vulnerable to North Korea's otherwise inferior conventional forces.
  - In a limited nuclear weapon attack on the ROK, even one weapon of the size of the North's fifth nuclear test could kill or seriously injure around half a million people in Seoul. A weapon the size of the North's sixth nuclear test could kill or seriously injure about 3 million people in either Seoul or New York City. Therefore, the ROK and the United States must strive to prevent North Korea from launching even one of these weapons (let alone many) at the ROK or the United States.
  - Even if North Korea never launches nuclear weapons, it likely would use its possession of nuclear weapons to coerce especially the ROK; to undermine U.S. extended deterrence provided to the ROK; and to decouple the ROK-U.S. alliance.

- North Korea cannot give up its nuclear weapons or infrastructure if it wants to accomplish its principal objectives. It likely will not even accept a nuclear weapon production freeze. North Korea is presenting the ROK and the United States with a mid- to long-term nuclear weapon threat that negotiations are unlikely to solve.

Outlining the Proposed 2027 ROK and U.S. Strategy

The North Korean nuclear weapon threats present the ROK and the United States with a major quandary. The severity of the threat should force the ROK and the United States to do everything possible to stop the growth of the threat and to eliminate as many North Korean nuclear weapons as possible. But with negotiations having absolutely failed to accomplish these objectives, the ROK and the United States must now turn their attention to deterring North Korean nuclear weapon attacks and being able to defeat such attacks if deterrence fails. The ancient Roman general Vegetius wrote, "If you want peace, prepare for war."[2] The ROK and the United States must prepare to fight and win a war on the Korean Peninsula under conditions of North Korean nuclear weapon use, and both countries must be prepared to implement the current U.S. policy of destroying the Kim regime if it uses nuclear weapons. Although the

---

2   David, 2014.

ROK and the United States do not want to fight a war with North Korea, especially a nuclear war, at some point the North could still initiate such a conflict, especially if it becomes desperate and risk-acceptant. North Korea is providing the ROK and the United States with no option other than a major effort focused on deterrence and defense.

This chapter proposes such a strategy in three parts against a potential 2027 North Korean nuclear weapon threat of roughly 200 nuclear weapons and the missiles required to deliver them. The ROK and U.S. effort is lagging behind the development of the North Korean threat and, therefore, needs to start now, even if North Korea does not reach this threat level until 2030 or 2040. The three parts of the strategy are as follows.

Policy and Strategy Focused on ROK and U.S. Prevention Efforts to Deter, Defeat, Defend Against, and Dissuade North Korea

To support development of this policy, we propose the establishment of a "Team of Strategic Advisers" to better develop these concepts. Although defeating North Korean aggression would include substantial reliance on conventional force operations, this subject is outside the scope of this piece and, therefore, is addressed only in the context of securing conventional force survival in a nuclear weapon environment.

Capability Acquisition

This includes better assembly of information on the North Korean threat, better defensive capabilities, and better counterforce and counter-leadership strike capabilities.

Other Recommendations

Other recommendations include structured negotiations with North Korea that provide balanced exchanges; reevaluated conditions for OPCON transition; closer partnership between the ROK, the United States, and Japan; and information operations against North Korea.

A comprehensive defense against North Korean nuclear weapon use would cost more than the ROK and the United States are likely willing to pay; therefore, we outline options available for countering the North Korean threat. In many of these actions, the United States can expect Chinese resistance. Therefore, we conclude by describing how China might intervene and what the ROK and the United States should consider doing about likely Chinese actions.

Key ROK and U.S. Strategy: Deter, Defeat, Defend, and Dissuade North Korea

U.S. national security doctrine focuses on deterring adversary nuclear weapon threats. According to the 2018 *Nuclear Posture Review,* "The highest U.S. nuclear policy and strategy priority is to deter potential adversaries from nuclear attack of any scale."[3] Accomplishing this and other objectives requires serious pursuit of the four activities described in this section. Deter, defeat, defend, and dissuade are not mutually distinct concepts, but rather are heavily interwoven. Nevertheless, addressing each provides insights into the desired ROK and U.S. strategy.

Deterrence and Imposing Costs

According to the 2006 U.S. Department of Defense *Deterrence Operations Joint Operating Concept,* "Deterrence operations convince adversaries not to take actions that threaten US vital interests by means of decisive influence over their decision-making. Decisive influence is achieved by credibly threatening to deny benefits and/or impose costs . . . ."[4] In simple terms, it is expected that the adversary will be deterred if the benefits that he hopes to achieve will not be worth the costs that he must withstand in trying to achieve those benefits, as shown in Figure 5.1. This means that if the ROK and the United States can clearly defeat North Korea, denying North Korea the benefits it seeks while punishing it with serious costs, then North Korea likely will be deterred. The *defend* concept is also critical in denying the benefits that North Korea seeks.

Much of the literature equates deterrence with the punishment aspect of this framework. Although nuclear deterrence historically has placed significant emphasis on imposing cost through the strategy of assured destruction (destroying an adversary's cities and population so that the society is no longer viable), current U.S. strategy takes a different approach toward North Korea:

> Our deterrence strategy for North Korea makes clear that any North Korean nuclear attack against the United States or its allies and partners is unacceptable and will result in the end of that regime. There is no scenario in which the Kim regime could employ nuclear weapons and survive.[5]

Because the North Korean regime is focused on its own survival, regime elimination is an appropriate focus for imposing costs. If successful, it would also decapitate

---

[3]   U.S. Department of Defense, 2018b, p. 7.

[4]   This quote is simplified; it does not mention adversary restraint, which can also be important. See U.S. Department of Defense, *Deterrence Operations Joint Operating Concept,* Version 2.0, Washington, D.C., December 2006, p. 8.

[5]   U.S. Department of Defense, 2018b, p. 33.

Figure 5.1
The Deterrence Framework

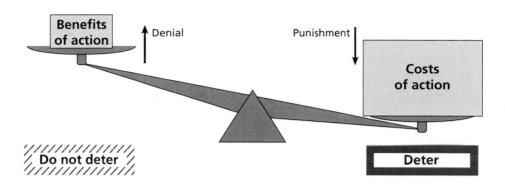

the nuclear weapon command and control system, potentially preventing the benefits North Korea would seek from using nuclear weapons by aborting many of North Korea's launches. The ROK refers to its ability to accomplish this objective as *overwhelming response*.[6] However, today, the U.S. threat of regime elimination has two major failings: (1) No strategy is described for eliminating the North Korean regime, and (2) this U.S. threat is not mentioned in most U.S. national security documents.[7]

Analysts expect that if North Korea ever launches a nuclear weapon, the regime itself will be hidden in a protected and deep underground facility.[8] According to the U.S. National Academies, "Many of the more important strategic hard and deeply buried targets are beyond the reach of conventional explosive penetrating weapons and can be held at risk of destruction only with nuclear weapons."[9] Historically, the United States has feared that its nuclear attacks against deeply buried targets would create immense amounts of fallout that might cause problems as far away as Japan. But the United States has learned that the nuclear yield required to destroy a deeply buried facility would reduce by a factor of 15 to 25 if a nuclear weapon were detonated a few meters in the ground, enhancing ground shock coupling and substantially reduc-

---

[6]   The ROK plans to target the regime outside its deeply buried facilities. It initially referred to this capability as *Korean Massive Punishment and Retaliation*, but it now calls it *overwhelming response* (Noh Ji-won, "Defense Ministry Changes Terminology for 'Three-Axis System' of Military Response," *Hankyoreh*, January 13, 2019).

[7]   Arguably, these "failures" might be part of U.S. "calculated ambiguity," which the United States has used to avoid committing to specific responses to an attack on itself or its allies. Against a risk-adverse adversary, such an approach to deterrence preserves U.S. flexibility while still being a largely effective deterrent. But against a risk-taker like North Korea, and especially if the North Korean regime fears that it is facing rebellion inside North Korea, ambiguity could undermine ROK and U.S. deterrence credibility.

[8]   See, for example, Moon Sung-hwi, "North Korea Moves Its Wartime Command Center to Nampo Taesan," *Liberty Korea Post*, July 7, 2018.

[9]   National Research Council, *Effects of Nuclear Earth-Penetrator and Other Weapons*, Washington, D.C.: The National Academies Press, 2005, p. 1.

ing the collateral damage caused by both the prompt and fallout effects. Successfully eliminating the North Korean regime would thus require ROK and U.S. knowledge of the regime location (at least narrowed down to a small number of facilities); U.S. use of precision conventional weapons against potential aboveground and shallow underground locations; and probably several earth-penetrating nuclear weapons against each potential deep underground location, as discussed later. By more broadly announcing this strategy, the United States would be more likely to convince Kim that the U.S. threat of regime destruction is real, making North Korean nuclear weapon use highly dangerous to the regime. However, the United States must be clear about whether this threat applies to both major and limited nuclear weapon use by North Korea,[10] and how the United States would respond to limited nuclear attacks not covered by this threat. Such explanations also would give the ROK a high-probability nuclear response assurance, which many ROK national security experts think is critical for deterring North Korean nuclear weapon use.

Another key to deterring North Korea is the willingness of the United States to meet this commitment in any circumstance in which North Korea launches a nuclear weapon. In a major crisis, North Korea might test the U.S. resolve by launching a missile with a nuclear weapon in a demonstration, causing little damage. North Korea could then gradually escalate nuclear weapon use in the way that it sometimes does with its provocations, seeking to condition the United States and being prepared to disengage once the United States becomes more serious about retaliation. The United States would undermine nuclear deterrence globally by allowing this to happen. Instead, the United States must be clear that it will do just what its threat says, laying out the U.S. nuclear retaliation strategy for fulfilling this threat against regime locations to be identified. One of the most powerful ways to deter North Korea would be to periodically tell the regime the location of Kim Jong-un, demonstrating an ability to target him despite his efforts to hide.

Preparing to Defeat North Korea

As noted earlier, the best ways to avoid a nuclear war with North Korea are to prepare for it and to demonstrate to North Korea that it cannot win such a conflict, even if it uses nuclear weapons. The logic of deterrence suggests that if North Korea clearly recognizes that it cannot benefit from the use of nuclear weapons, it probably will be deterred from using them—and, with some exceptions (such as nuclear weapon tests), that has been the case thus far. But North Korea would not be paying

---

[10] For example, would the U.S. President be prepared to eliminate the North Korean regime, killing tens of thousands of North Koreans or more in the process, if the North does a nuclear weapon test on a ballistic missile launched over the East Sea (the Sea of Japan)? If not, then to deter such an action, the United States needs to explain what it would do in such a case. The United States often relies on deterrence by ambiguity, but North Korea likely will continue to test ambiguous U.S. deterrence threats as it has in the past, making such ambiguous deterrents relatively useless in the end.

high development costs and sanctions penalties if it did not believe that, with enough nuclear weapons, it could benefit from their use or threats of their use. Now that North Korea apparently has dozens of nuclear weapons and is building toward hundreds, the ROK and the United States should consider significantly enhancing their counter-leadership capabilities to decapitate North Korean nuclear command and control to avoid nuclear weapon launches, consistent with the U.S. deterrent threat that the regime will not survive if it uses nuclear weapons (decapitation could be aided by appropriate cyberattacks).[11]

The U.S. deterrent threat that the regime will not survive nuclear weapon use is a powerful threat, but the uncertainties in carrying out that threat (especially being able to locate the regime) might undermine deterrence and be insufficient to convince North Korea that it cannot win a war. North Korea likely will question its ability to win a war with the ROK and the United States if they have the capabilities to destroy most of the North Korean nuclear weapons with a series of counterforce attacks on North Korean missile fields and nuclear weapon storage before the missiles can be launched,[12] preventing the launch of these weapons even if the North's command and control somehow survives.

Recognizing that attempts to destroy the North Korean command system and nuclear weapons could still be imperfect, the ROK and the United States would need defensive capabilities sufficient to intercept and destroy most of the North Korean missiles carrying nuclear weapons that could survive and be launched.[13] The ROK has discussed establishing a "three-axis system" of counter-leadership targeting, counterforce targeting, and defensive measures to defeat North Korean nuclear forces. However, the United States has avoided any significant discussion of its counter-leadership and counterforce capabilities against North Korea. With an aggressive country like North Korea, the United States needs to take a more proactive defense approach to clearly convey to the North the U.S. commitment to extended deterrence and offensive action against it if it ever uses a nuclear weapon (and this would also reassure many in the ROK). Indeed, the ROK and the United States should tell North Korea (and China) that North Korean nuclear weapon use would make any Korean war a total conflict (not a limited conflict) in which the ROK and U.S. objective would be the destruction of the North Korean regime, followed by ROK-led unification.

The biggest risk to ROK security would occur if the ROK-U.S. alliance were somehow decoupled. Therefore, decoupling the alliance has become a major North Korean objective. Without the U.S. extended deterrence guarantee, the ROK would

---

[11] Ankit Panda, *Kim Jong Un and the Bomb: Survival and Deterrence in North Korea*, New York: Oxford University Press, 2020, pp. 240–243.

[12] The ROK has referred to this capability as its *kill chain*, although the Moon administration refers to it as *Strategic Target Strike* (Noh, 2019).

[13] The ROK has referred to this capability as *Korean Air and Missile Defense*.

be extremely vulnerable to North Korean nuclear weapon coercion and use, something to be strongly avoided. In such a case, it is entirely possible that the ROK would conclude that it needs a crash nuclear weapons program and that it might have the nuclear materials and human capital required to develop nuclear weapons relatively promptly. The United States needs to avoid such an outcome by strengthening the alliance, as U.S. President Joe Biden has promised to do.[14]

Defending the ROK and the United States

An ROK and U.S. ability to defeat North Korea does not guarantee an acceptable level of ROK and U.S. survival in a nuclear conflict. North Korean use of even a few dozen nuclear weapons early in the conflict could substantially negate major ROK and U.S. military advantages, such as airpower, that are based on fixed facilities that could be targeted with North Korean nuclear weapons. As the number of North Korean nuclear weapons and their capabilities grow, ROK and U.S. military survivability becomes an increasingly serious concern.

Defense allows the ROK and the United States to reduce the damage that North Korea can cause with its nuclear weapons, denying North Korea some of the benefits of those weapons. Defense capabilities thus strengthen deterrence, but they also support the ROK and the United States should deterrence fail. Over the past two decades, much of the defense against adversary nuclear weapon use has focused on air and missile defense—i.e., seeking to shoot down aircraft and missiles that might attempt to deliver nuclear weapons against the ROK or the United States. These capabilities remain important, but there are various other ways of defending against adversary use of nuclear weapons, many of which were developed by both the North Atlantic Treaty Organization (NATO) and the Warsaw Pact during the Cold War. These include the use of dispersal bases, hardening of key facilities, denial of North Korean intelligence on targets, and force mobility that reduces the effectiveness of North Korean nuclear targeting.

For example, there are only about a dozen combat airfields in the ROK. Today, North Korea could target those airfields with one or two missiles, each carrying a nuclear weapon. Although the unreliability of North Korean missiles and the effectiveness of ROK and U.S. missile defenses might eliminate many of those missiles before their nuclear weapons could detonate on the airfields, at least some of the airfields could be significantly damaged by the nuclear weapons. As the number of North Korean nuclear weapons increases to allow for three or four or five missiles to be fired at each airfield, more of the airfields are likely to be damaged. During the Cold War, both the United States and the Soviet Union developed dispersal airfields to which fighter aircraft could be sent and where they could then operate with much less likelihood of being successfully targeted. Korea also has locations that could be used for

---

[14] Joe Biden, "Hope for Our Better Future," Yonhap News Agency, October 29, 2020.

aircraft dispersal in a conflict. The ROK Air Force could provide modest spending for the supplies and manpower needed to operate dispersed aircraft at these locations.[15]

Additionally, the allies should explore options to minimize damage to the ROK's civilian population. This is especially true in response to the North Korean threat to "destroy the Earth," mentioned in previous chapters. The ROK already plans to protect its urban population in the existing subways. A study from the Asan Institute for Policy Studies in Seoul estimated that more than 1.8 million civilians, representing 3.5 percent of the total population, would not be able to access adequate evacuation facilities on the first day of the conflict, and 6.5 million people (12.7 percent of the total population) would not find adequate shelter for medium-term requirements after two or three days.[16] Another option would be evacuation of urban areas; some of this evacuation likely would occur spontaneously, as warning of war built. Neglecting to protect a high number of civilians could lead to massive casualties and to weakening of the resolve to respond decisively, thereby undermining the allies' determination to continue fighting. Therefore, significantly increasing the amount of shelter space for civilian protection and arranging for systematic urban evacuation should be considered as part of the defensive plan against North Korea's nuclear weapon use.

Dissuade

North Korea apparently builds nuclear weapons because it perceives that those weapons could have significant utility for the North Korean regime. The term *dissuade* means to convince North Korea that nuclear weapons do not have such utility—that they are actually a liability, and that the North should limit and reduce its investments in nuclear weapons. The ROK and the United States clearly have failed to do this, allowing North Korea to think that expanding its nuclear weapon force will provide the regime considerable utility.

To convince North Korea that it does not have much to gain from nuclear weapons, the ROK and the United States need to field substantial counter–nuclear weapon capabilities coupled with more-active threats to demonstrate the ROK and U.S. will to defeat North Korea and destroy the regime if it ever employs a nuclear weapon. As these capabilities develop, the ROK and the United States also need to carry out an active information operations campaign so that the North Korean regime understands the jeopardy associated with its nuclear weapons and understands that its investments

---

[15] In practice, the ROK had many highway landing strips designed to operate as dispersal airfields years ago. Many of them have since been abandoned, the ROK not expecting a serious threat against its airfields. The growth in North Korean nuclear weapons has reinstated this threat and requires an ROK Air Force effort to reevaluate potential dispersal airfields. In addition, the ROK has a reasonable number of modestly sized airports that could be used for fighter dispersal.

[16] J. James Kim, Kim Chong Woo, Kim Seonkyung, and Ham Geon Hee, *Assessing South Korea's Civil Defense Emergency Evacuation Facilities*, Seoul, South Korea: Asan Institute for Policy Studies, April 3, 2018.

in nuclear weapons are a waste of money.[17] Former ROK President Park Geun-hye described this objective:

> While maintaining strong (South) Korea-U.S. joint defense system, the government will secure anti-weapons of mass destruction capabilities, such as kill chain and the Korea Air and Missile Defense (KAMD) system, at an early date to make North Korea realize on its own that its nuclear weapons and missiles . . . are useless.[18]

As we explained in the earlier chapters, North Korea apparently hopes that a large number of nuclear weapons would allow it to discredit the U.S. extended deterrence guarantee, break the ROK-U.S. alliance, and either coerce the ROK into unification or conquer the ROK. Because North Korean ICBMs with nuclear weapons would threaten the U.S. ability to maintain this guarantee, the United States needs to prioritize having adequate missile defense of the United States. However, U.S. missile defense was always intended to cover just a small ICBM threat from Iran and North Korea, not to grow so large as to counter the Russian or Chinese ICBM threat to the United States, thereby destabilizing strategic deterrence. At some level of growth of the North Korean ICBM threat, the United States will not be able to continue to expand its homeland missile defense and still maintain this balance. A U.S. development of more-serious offensive capabilities (as discussed later) might convince North Korea to limit the growth of its ICBM forces and also might give China incentives to pressure North Korea to discontinue the growth of its ICBMs.

If North Korea were to conclude that its nuclear weapons are mainly useless and actually dangerous to the regime, it might well be dissuaded from building more nuclear weapons and might even decide to surrender some that it already has.

Preparing and Refining ROK and U.S. Strategy for Nuclear Warfare
It has generally been assumed that in a major Korean conflict, any nuclear weapon use on either side would be limited and would not fundamentally interfere with the conventional warfighting that CFC planned. Because the CFC staff were not trained to be experts in nuclear warfare, the nuclear planning could be performed by other organizations. However, as the North Korean nuclear weapon threat has grown, and especially as we project it to grow by 2027, any nuclear weapon use in Korea is likely to fundamentally affect the conventional military operations and, therefore, must become part of the CFC planning process—a fundamental application of the U.S. military concept of unity of command.

---

[17] More is said about the needed information operations campaign in a later section.

[18] "Park Pledges Strong Defense to Render N. Korean Nukes Useless," *Korea Herald*, October 1, 2013.

To provide the expert support for making this transition, we propose creating a combined "Team of Strategic Advisers" to support CFC in planning for combined nuclear and conventional operations. The ROK and the United States use many advisers to assist CFC in war planning, exercises, and other functions. This team of perhaps 15 to 20 U.S. and ROK experts would be tasked with providing the CFC staff with background understanding on nuclear weapons, their potential effects, and how they might be used by either side. The team likely would be derived from a combination of government personnel, academics, and military officers. In addition, the team likely would include some U.S. personnel who had experience in planning nuclear and conventional warfighting during the Cold War and, therefore, would be able to draw on lessons learned during that period. The advisers would support the CFC commander in developing appropriate strategy options for CFC and preparing initial plans to respond to integrated North Korean nuclear and conventional threats. In doing so, they would help assure the ROK side of the viability of the U.S. nuclear umbrella during a time in which there are increasing ROK doubts regarding U.S. extended deterrence. They would be a resource prepared to help adjust plans in an conflict based on the events actually experienced, and, in particular, they would prepare the CFC staff to use nuclear weapons against time-urgent targets. In addition, they would be particularly important in helping the ROK side prepare to take the lead in such planning after OPCON transfer, subject to the limits on disclosing U.S. nuclear weapon information to the ROK.

As the North Korean nuclear weapon threat has grown, there has already been increasing interest among the ROK military and broader national security community to understand nuclear weapons and associated strategy and policies. Several ROK and U.S. committees have been created to provide some of the information required by the ROK side, and, in particular, the ROK-U.S. Extended Deterrence Policy Committee led to the preparation of several useful combined concepts. In preparing for OPCON transfer, some U.S. officials have assumed that an ROK commander of CFC would simply let his U.S. deputy handle coordination of nuclear weapon use. This could happen, but our experience suggests that the ROK CFC commander will probably want to develop his own strategy for countering North Korean nuclear weapon use and to nominate nuclear targets and converse with the U.S. President about releasing and using those nuclear weapons.[19] Indeed, according to interviews conducted in

---

[19] By analogy, in the aftermath of North Korea's sinking of an ROK warship and shelling of an ROK island in 2010, the ROK developed its own "proactive deterrence strategy" and augmented it with new concepts over time, often without prior consultation or only limited consultation with the U.S. government. In addition, despite the ROK military subordination within CFC, in 2013, the ROK defense ministry told the National Assembly that, if faced with a North Korean use of nuclear weapons, "the South Korean military would react proactively to a contingency without consulting U.S. forces by exercising its right to self-defense" (Ser Myo-ja, "Park Tells Military to Strike Back If Attacked," *JoongAng Daily*, April 1, 2013). The ROK chairman of the joint chiefs of staff "made clear that preemptive strikes on the North's nuclear facilities are a matter of exercising the right of self-defense and Seoul does not require Washington's consent to make them" (Ser, 2013).

Seoul in 2017, the ROK defense ministry has already made some efforts to develop ROK nuclear warfare strategy but has been hampered by a lack of ROK experts on nuclear weapons use and deterrence. In addition, the ROK president might well insist on reviewing and approving any nuclear weapon use against North Korea, and there could be potentially serious consequences after a conflict termination if that does not happen. A Team of Strategic Advisors could provide background information and help set up procedures to make all of this work.[20] Indeed, this basic concept was considered by the ROK defense minister several years ago and was approved because he was anxious to bring this expertise and planning to the ROK military, but the U.S. side never finalized the concept.

What Capabilities Should the ROK and the United States Be Developing?

The ROK and the United States have done much to prepare for defeating a conventional North Korean military attack, and many of those preparations carry over to nuclear conflict. But there are also other areas in which ROK and U.S. capabilities are insufficient for dealing with North Korean nuclear weapon attacks. The allies must significantly enhance their capabilities in these areas to gain the leverage required for strong deterrence. Many of the enhanced capabilities can be achieved at limited cost, especially in areas in which strategy and operational concepts can be adjusted, and these changes are obvious priorities. Other changes will require moderate to significant expenses, especially in acquiring new equipment; the ROK and the United States need to make some more-difficult choices on which of these changes to make.

Target Information
To mount effective counterforce and counter-leadership attacks, the ROK and the United States need to identify the location and status of the North Korean leaders, their nuclear weapons, and their ballistic missiles. Identifying the location of North Korea's nuclear weapons might be easier than some might expect:

> In North Korea, nuclear warheads are not mated in peacetime with their ballistic missiles, and this requisite step for launch is a form of check and verification. . . . North Korea operates a single storage site for its manufactured warheads and their

---

[20] Some ROK security experts talk about forming a counterpart to the NATO Nuclear Planning Group, which was begun in 1966 to bring non-U.S. personnel into the NATO nuclear planning process. See, for example, Timothy Andrews Sayle, "A Nuclear Education: The Origins of NATO's Nuclear Planning Group," *Journal of Strategic Studies*, Vol. 43, No. 6–7, 2020.

fissile cores: an underground facility known to the United States as Yongdoktong, northeast of the city of Kusong.[21]

Kim has probably chosen this approach because he does not trust his military and wants centralized control of the nuclear weapons, reducing the chances that these weapons would be used against him.[22] Interestingly, China apparently used a similar approach for similar reasons.[23]

Of course, North Korea could change this approach at any time, which would require that the ROK and the United States have the ability to identify potentially multiple North Korean nuclear weapon storage sites and many ballistic missile locations. This could be particularly challenging because North Korea endeavors to deny the ROK and the United States targeting information on the locations of the regime's personnel, nuclear weapons, and delivery platforms.

Increasing ROK and U.S. intelligence collection with satellites, aircraft, and drones will be a natural part of this effort. Therefore, one ROK and U.S. option is to increase the use of these assets, and another is to acquire more of these assets, especially advanced versions. However, even more important might be obtaining information from North Koreans to cue this reconnaissance. For example, disaffected North Korean officers might suggest that the TELs for ballistic missiles have been seen in certain areas or that Kim visited a particular facility on a given day. Getting such information from within North Korea or motivating appropriate defections will not be easy, but ROK and U.S. information operations might motivate some North Koreans to attempt to provide information. Human intelligence would also be important in identifying when North Korea is preparing to use its nuclear forces so that a preemptive, or at least time-urgent, attack could be carried out. Of course, North Korean security services will try to send false information, but identifying some intelligence information as being false is a normal part of intelligence collection.

A combined intelligence system already exists for the ROK and the United States. However, this information is not always shared, because of fear that too much exposure might reveal the identity of sensitive sources. Still, efforts should be made to share key information and make it as comprehensive, coordinated, and reliable as possible, especially to support ROK and U.S. preemptive actions. An inexpensive way to enhance coordination would be to run regular command post exercises that simulate counterforce attacks on North Korea. These exercises could identify information gaps and allow follow-up efforts to prioritize information collection to fill those gaps. Coor-

---

[21] Panda, 2020, pp. 244–245.

[22] In a March 2017 interview, a very senior North Korean military defector and escapee said that Kim had ordered that no chemical weapons were to be stored within artillery range of Pyongyang because he did not feel that he could trust all of his military.

[23] Mark A. Stokes, *China's Nuclear Warhead Storage and Handling System*, Arlington, Va.: Project 2049 Institute, March 12, 2010.

dination of analysis and judgment is also required to secure shared ROK and U.S. situational awareness.

Preparation to Defeat North Korean Nuclear Warfare

ROK and U.S. conventional force superiority makes clear that North Korea would lose any conflict in which it did not use nuclear weapons. The result of conventional superiority has been a period of almost 70 years during which the ROK and the United States have deterred North Korea from major conventional warfare. But North Korea's pursuit of substantial numbers of nuclear weapons suggests that the ROK and the United States have not deterred North Korea from considering nuclear warfare. The proposed Team of Strategic Advisers should recommend actions that the United States can take to defeat North Korean nuclear weapon attacks and reassure the ROK and other regional partners by putting all options on the table, to include (1) dedicating U.S. strategic nuclear weapons or nuclear platforms, or both, to targeting North Korea;[24] (2) deploying the planned U.S. intermediate-range ballistic missiles with nuclear weapons in or near the ROK;[25] and (3) deploying U.S. tactical nuclear weapons in Korea.

In addition, it is surprising that the ROK and the United States maintain military infrastructure in the ROK that is probably adequate for conventional warfare but does not provide adequate protections for nuclear warfare in Korea. This difference is illustrated by the fact that there is only a small number (about a dozen) of combat air bases in the ROK. Moreover, few military bases in the ROK include shelters and other protections against nuclear weapons or maintain constant dispersal of parts of their forces.[26]

Improving these conditions will be a moderate expense that will be required to convince North Korea that the ROK and the United States are indeed prepared to defeat it in nuclear warfare. Unless the ROK and the United States visibly organize, plan, and train for nuclear warfare (including in their war plans and major exercises), North Korea may conclude that it can win such a conflict, undermining deterrence. Relatively few ROK and U.S. military officers are familiar with nuclear weapons and how they would affect warfare in Korea; the proposed Team of Strategic Advisers could provide basic nuclear weapon information to these personnel as needed in addition to more-advanced coordination of nuclear employment planning with selected ROK and U.S. personnel. Planning for nuclear warfare in Korea must focus on nuclear

---

[24] By analogy, during the Cold War, the United States dedicated to NATO 400 nuclear warheads on Poseidon strategic submarines (Milton Leitenberg, *Studies of Military R&D and Weapons Development*, Center for International and Security Studies, University of Maryland, 1984, p. 17).

[25] For example, see Ellen Mitchell, "Pentagon Chief says US Looking to Put Intermediate-Range Missiles in Asia," *The Hill*, August 3, 2019.

[26] In fact, the U.S. military in Korea has consolidated its military bases, seeking efficient and personnel-friendly conditions. The tension between these conditions and military protection needs to be reexamined in an era with a serious North Korean nuclear weapon threat.

clarity—making planned U.S. nuclear responses clear—rather than the historical nuclear ambiguity from which the United States could well withdraw. In addition, extensive ROK and U.S. analysis and gaming of nuclear conflict would identify gaps to CFC that could be resolved and thereby enhance capabilities. These changes would not be expensive.

In addition, the UNC has become more important because of the increasing North Korean nuclear threats and the decline in the size of the ROK's military. The UNC performs a critical role as a force and facility provider in case of a contingency on the Korean Peninsula. The UNC should be strengthened to fully perform its functions, even in conjunction with a North Korean surprise nuclear weapon attack. In particular, given the damage that North Korean nuclear weapons could do to ROK and U.S. facilities on the peninsula, arrangements to use UNC off-peninsula facilities as fallback operating locations should be reinforced. The UN's sending states could also be helpful in providing forces that could replace ROK and U.S. personnel lost to nuclear weapon attacks, although many sending states could be reluctant to offer bases or forces until the North's nuclear weapon threat is suppressed (making that effort even more important). This likely would require more participation of the sending states in peninsula exercises and other activities. North Korean nuclear attacks against the forces or citizens of the nuclear sending states (the United Kingdom and France)[27] could lead them to want to retaliate against North Korea with nuclear weapons.

Better Defensive Capabilities
There are various options by which the ROK and the United States could upgrade their forces and cities for protection against nuclear weapon effects.[28] The ROK and the United States could increase the level of resilience by developing dispersal options, as discussed earlier, and making command and control and logistics more redundant to cope with potential losses. The defense against chemical and biological weapons and conventional attacks could also be enhanced—North Korea can be expected to exploit any gap in the ROK and U.S. defenses. ROK and U.S. missile defenses could be better protected and more capable; this would include more-thorough integration of ROK missile defenses into the U.S. missile defense system. The ROK and the United States should also expect that North Korea would use substantial cyber warfare capabilities to attack them before and during a nuclear conflict, and they need to consider enhancing their protection against such penetrations. ROK and U.S. cyber experts are probably

---

[27] According to the Korean Immigration Service, there were 5,980 French citizens and 7,550 UK citizens living in the ROK at the end of 2019 (Korea Immigration Service, *2019 Statistical Yearbook of Immigration and Foreigners Policy*, July 13, 2020).

[28] The ROK has assumed that its subway systems would be an appropriate shelter for its civilian population, and that is true relative to conventional artillery or missile threats. However, against nuclear weapons, the subways would require blast doors, which few of the subway stations in Seoul appear to include.

already monitoring North Korean attempts to install means for damaging ROK and U.S. infrastructure and hopefully can identify and neutralize many of those means.

Long ago, the ROK and the United States concluded that a North Korean invasion of the ROK had to end with the ROK and the United States capturing the North and absorbing it into the ROK to prevent a repeat North Korean attack within a few years. The presence of North Korean WMD in the North requires special ROK and U.S. efforts to eliminate the WMD during the ROK and U.S. operations in the North. Unfortunately, the severe reductions planned in the ROK Army's active-duty manpower might not provide adequate capability for such operations in the future, unless a significant number of the ROK Army reserves are trained more than just three days per year and prepared to play a major role in capturing the North.

Counterforce and Counter-Leadership Strike Capabilities

At some number of North Korean nuclear weapon and missile capabilities, ROK and U.S. defenses will become inadequate to counter the North Korean threat. This is especially true for the defense of the U.S. homeland, which is purposefully sized for only limited threats so as not to imperil the Russian and Chinese nuclear deterrents that sustain strategic nuclear weapon stability. The ROK and the United States should establish numbers of North Korean nuclear weapons and delivery means at which ROK and U.S. defenses begin losing adequacy, and they should warn North Korea that if it crosses these defense inadequacy thresholds, the ROK and the United States will be forced to vigorously pursue counterforce and counter-leadership attack capabilities to counter the growing North Korean threat. At first, North Korea is unlikely to believe that the ROK and the United States are serious about these thresholds; as North Korea approaches them, the ROK and the United States need to increase the efforts that they expend on building counterforce and counter-leadership attack capabilities. China will also be sensitive about ROK and U.S. capability increases around these thresholds and might put pressure on North Korea to stay below these thresholds to avoid a significant expansion of ROK and U.S. capabilities.

Building ROK and U.S. counterforce and counter-leadership capabilities will be expensive but required to deny North Korea leverage against the ROK and the United States with its growing nuclear weapon force. Plans for the ROK kill chain system include the diverse capabilities required for counterforce and counter-leadership targeting for both countries. Many of the North Korean nuclear and leadership targets will be time urgent, and, therefore, the ROK and the United States should depend on ballistic missiles for the first stage of the attacks.[29] The United States has a significant shortage of theater ballistic missiles deployed on and around the Korean Peninsula and

---

[29] Kim Sang-hyup, "South Korea and the United States Build Precision Strikes in the 5th Stage of North Korean Anti-Missiles," *Munhwa Ilbo*, October 10, 2012.

is beginning to build such delivery systems.[30] The ROK and the United States also need precision conventional munitions for attacking the North Korean targets that are not deeply buried, with sufficient numbers to cover all potential targets that cannot be ruled out and to restrike targets not killed in the first attack stage. In addition, fighter aircraft or drones, or both, will be required to search for North Korean mobile targets and strike them promptly once they are discovered.[31]

Offensive cyber warfare and special forces might be ideal for neutralizing or destroying some of the North Korean targets while limiting collateral damage. Even though North Korea attempts to maintain a largely closed cyber system, ROK and U.S. cyber experts likely have the ability to penetrate the North Korean nuclear command and control system and prevent or delay some launch orders from being transmitted, at least until ROK and U.S. counterforce strikes can be delivered.

As noted earlier, the United States likely will want to keep secure most of its nuclear weapons that are dedicated to North Korean targets, probably on a ballistic missile submarine at sea. The United States also might want to keep some dual-capable aircraft available on Korean airfields for nuclear weapon delivery, since the U.S. weapon that appears best for use against North Korea's deep underground facilities is the B61-12, with its low yield (minimizing collateral damage) and earth-penetrating capabilities.[32]

As the number of North Korean nuclear weapons grows, North Korea will be able to do more damage to the ROK and the United States, and defeating North Korean nuclear weapon use will become more difficult and costly. Ironically, North Korea would thus force the ROK and the United States to emphasize more counterforce and counter-leadership targeting early in a campaign. To apply pressure on North Korea, the United States should establish thresholds of North Korean nuclear weapons (maybe 80 to 100), and especially ICBM inventory (maybe 15 to 25), at which

1. the United States would deploy in the ROK a small number (maybe eight to ten) of B61-12 tactical nuclear bombs for destroying deeply buried leadership facilities and four or so U.S. dual-capable fighter aircraft for delivering them[33]

---

[30] See Mitchell, 2019.

[31] This mode of operating is referred to as *armed reconnaissance*.

[32] National Research Council, 2005, p. 2. For example, the new B61-12 tactical nuclear weapon reportedly has a yield of 50 KT, yet if it penetrates roughly 3 m into the ground before detonating, "the maximum destructive potential of the B61-12 against underground targets is equivalent to the capability of a surface-burst weapon with a yield of 750 kt to 1,250 kt" (Hans M. Kristensen and Matthew McKinzie, "Video Shows Earth-Penetrating Capability of B61-12 Nuclear Bomb," Federation of American Scientists, January 14, 2016). A number of ROK experts have encouraged the United States to return tactical nuclear weapons to the peninsula.

[33] If North Korea uses a nuclear weapon, the United States will want to execute a decapitation attack on Kim rapidly and perhaps even preemptively. Nuclear weapons based in the United States likely cannot be used in such a manner—it would take too long to deploy the weapons and the dual-capable aircraft to the ROK. But a station-

2. the United States would transition to a preemptive concept of operation for counterforce and counter-leadership targeting.[34]

Although the second recommendation might seem radical, it fits within the scope of Vice Chairman of the Joint Chiefs of Staff General John E. Hyten's recent admonition that, "when you look at missile defense and missile defeat, it's important to look at the entire kill chain, and instead of starting from the back end, where Patriot works in a point defense system, it's important to think about how you defeat and defend left of launch first."[35] The phrase *left of launch* means before North Korea would launch; this would be a preemptive operation.

A U.S. threat to put the B61-12s in the ROK would make the U.S. threat of regime destruction more prompt and credible and would help emphasize to North Korea that it needs to implement a nuclear weapon freeze to avoid this serious threat. Similarly, a transition to planning preemptive counterforce and counter-leadership targeting would put the North at greater risk and hopefully push it into a nuclear weapon production freeze, although this transition also could have a serious destabilizing effect on Northeast Asia.

There is a risk that taking such strong ROK and U.S. actions will sustain or even enhance North Korean hostility. If so, North Korea could be more inclined to quicken the pace of its nuclear weapon program and commit more provocations. Because the North already appears to be expending enormous resources on its nuclear weapon program, it likely cannot do much beyond ongoing efforts to increase its nuclear weapon buildup. But North Korean provocations would increase regional tensions, which would also upset China and Russia. The ROK and the United States would need to mount a major information operation explaining that the North is fully responsible both for the ROK and U.S. increased defenses and for any increased North Korean provocations. They would need to seek Chinese and Russian support to at least freeze North Korean nuclear weapon and ballistic missile production and thereby reduce tensions. A rollback of North Korean nuclear weapons and ICBMs to the established ROK and U.S. thresholds would cause the U.S. nuclear weapons deployed to the ROK to be returned to the United States, and the preemptive planning would be terminated.

---

ing of even eight to ten B61-12s in the ROK should be sufficient for a time-urgent decapitation attack, allowing the United States to protect the rest of these weapons in the United States while still being able to deploy the remainder for prolonged counter-leadership targeting, if needed.

[34] Such actions, coupled with fielding adequate missile defenses and offensive counterforce capabilities, likely will be critical to demonstrating that the United States sustains a capability to protect its homeland against North Korean nuclear weapon attacks even as the North Korean threat grows.

[35] John E. Hyten, "Missile Defense and Defeat: A Conversation with the Vice Chairman," transcript of webinar on February 23, 2021, Center for Strategic and International Studies, 2021, p. 4.

Other Recommendations for ROK and U.S. Strategy

Although Kim seems likely to retain some, and perhaps many, nuclear weapons regardless of what the ROK and the United States offer, the ROK and the United States should still be pursuing negotiations to slow, if not stop, the growth in North Korean nuclear weapons and, if possible, to reduce the number of weapons. In addition, the ROK and the United States should be countering the North Korean psychological operations that seek to depict the United States as the villain in Northeast Asia, and they should use information operations to strengthen the ROK-U.S. alliance, help the North Korean elites recognize the dangers of the North's nuclear weapons, and pressure the regime to freeze and roll back its nuclear weapon program.

Negotiating with North Korea

Kim will almost certainly never give up his nuclear weapons as long as he perceives that they give him substantial utility that he cannot achieve in other ways. Unfortunately, to date, U.S. denuclearization negotiations with North Korea have done far more to recognize North Korea as a nuclear weapon and important state than to achieve denuclearization. Ironically, in many ways, that recognition makes it more difficult to induce North Korean denuclearization, because it demonstrates to Kim how his nuclear weapons have enhanced both the internal and external perceptions of North Korean power, something that Kim wants very much.

Although negotiations cannot be expected to even rein in the North Korean nuclear weapon threat any time soon, the ROK and the United States need to be clear on what is possible. ROK President Moon Jae-in recently "claimed that Kim still had a 'clear willingness' to denuclearize . . . ,"[36] which is not our belief. However, although many people in the ROK hold the same view as President Moon, we recommend that the U.S. President test this view by telling Kim that the President needs him to demonstrate that he is serious about and capable of even minor denuclearization. The President could challenge Kim, saying something like this:

> A lot of my people are saying that you are not the all-powerful supreme leader of North Korea, and I need to prove them wrong. Very few Americans think they can trust you to give up your nuclear weapons, because you have not given up any yet, after almost three years. Public opinion in the United States matters—we have already given you a lot, and we cannot give you much more until you give up one or more nuclear weapons, with IAEA verification, as a symbol of your personal ability to denuclearize.

---

[36] Kim Tong-Hyung, "Moon Urges Biden to Learn from Trump's N. Korea Diplomacy," Associated Press, January 18, 2020.

Kim probably would be unwilling to destroy even one nuclear warhead, because many of his elites would view such an action as demonstrating serious weakness relative to the United States, and this would cause problems between Kim and his military. If Kim fails to destroy any of his nuclear weapons, the people of the ROK hopefully would begin to realize that Kim really is building more than a trivial nuclear weapon threat, undermining the belief in the ROK that the North Korean nuclear weapon threat can be resolved by just offering a few more concessions.[37] However, if Kim accepts, then meaningful negotiations might be possible.

Kim seems most likely to consider negotiating limits on his nuclear weapons when he recognizes that they are actually a deadly liability. This is unlikely to occur until the United States seriously targets him and North Korea more broadly with nuclear weapons. The ROK and the United States must convince Kim that his nuclear weapons are not the tools that will allow him to control Korean unification and make North Korea a regional great power, and, to do so, the United States must demonstrate a firm commitment to ROK security and to defeating the regime if it ever uses nuclear weapons. Kim also must come to recognize that his nuclear weapons and his other efforts will not cause the decoupling of the ROK-U.S. alliance that he seeks.

Today, Kim clearly does not have these perspectives. And, without determined and sincere ROK and U.S. information operations, capability development, and commitment, he is unlikely to develop them. Until he does, he will make Northeast Asia an increasingly dangerous place. At the very least, the ROK and the United States should argue for a North Korean nuclear weapon production freeze based on Kim's statement at the October 2020 military parade: "We have built a deterrent with which we can satisfactorily control and manage any military threats that we are facing or may face."[38] If Kim's nuclear weapon deterrent really is sufficient for any military threats now or in the future, he does not need to produce any more nuclear weapons at great financial and sanctions costs to his country and contrary to his commitments.

To make any progress with North Korea, the ROK and the United States require a comprehensive political warfare strategy that would start during peacetime. Within that strategy, the United States should take a "carrot and stick" approach. On the "carrot" side, the United States should offer specific sanction relaxation in exchange for specific North Korean denuclearization actions. As another example, the United States could invite about 20 North Korean graduate students to get a Ph.D. at some of the

---

[37] ROK President "Moon and his progressive supporters believe . . . that granting major concessions that meet North Korea's demands without requiring conditions can persuade North Korea to denuclearize" (Duyeon Kim, "Washington and Seoul Must Heal Their Alliance: Confronting North Korean and Chinese Aggression Requires It," *Foreign Affairs*, January 26, 2021).

[38] Jeongmin Kim, "Apologies, Tears and a 'War Deterrent': Top Quotes from Kim Jong Un's Speech," NK News, October 12, 2020.

best U.S. universities, perhaps in exchange for Kim eliminating one nuclear weapon.[39] In December 2019, Kim ordered top students at Kim Il-Sung University to get a Ph.D., apparently as part of a program "to help cultivate the next generation of leadership."[40] At the same time, Kim reportedly visited Kim Il-Sung University and ordered the professors to begin publishing papers in journals outside North Korea.[41] What better way for North Korea to make that happen than to send some graduate students to U.S. universities, where they would begin publishing as part of their graduate school responsibilities and then return to North Korea as professors? Because there would be a security risk to the United States for doing this, the United States likely would need to limit these students to majors in the social sciences, business, and the arts. Still, most North Korean graduate students able to speak English well enough to study in the United States would be members of senior-elite families in North Korea and would share their experiences with their family members, demonstrating the lack of U.S. hostility. Various other exchanges should also be pursued to convince the North Korean elites that they have nothing to fear from the United States. North Korea will want the United States to sign a peace agreement or an end-of-war agreement, but the United States should respond as discussed in the subsection titled "Information Operations Against North Korea" to make it clear that North Korea is the real impediment to peace.

On the "stick" side, the United States should insist that the sanctions are in place because of North Korean bad behavior and that, as soon as that behavior turns favorable, the sanctions will go away—North Korea need only cooperate. Because of the rapid growth expected in the number of North Korean nuclear weapons, a critical objective would be to obtain a nuclear weapon production freeze from North Korea. The United States should emphasize the fact that Kim has already committed to such a freeze, in the 2018 Panmunjom Declaration (as noted in Chapter Two)[42] and in his 2019 New Year's address.[43] Kim's violation of these previous commitments warrants further sanctions action, which might include introducing U.S. warships in the northern part of the Yellow Sea to intercept North Korean ships in violation of sanctions prohibiting ship-to-ship transfers. This U.S. action would infuriate China. Therefore, the United States could first offer China the opportunity to interdict the ship-to-ship transfers, telling China that, if it does not, the United States will.

---

[39] Senior North Korean refugees tell me that most senior-elite families want their children trained in the United States. If Kim refused to allow this to happen, they would be seriously upset with him.

[40] Kim Jeong Hun, "Kim Il Sung University Graduates Ordered into Doctoral Programs," Daily NK, December 23, 2019.

[41] Interview with a senior official at the ROK Ministry of Unification, December 2019.

[42] Moon Jae-in and Kim Jong-un, 2018.

[43] As noted earlier, Kim said, "We declared at home and abroad that we would neither make and test nuclear weapons any longer nor use and proliferate them" (Kim Jong-un, 2019).

An ROK and U.S. working group could be created to identify other ways to increase pressure against North Korea in a measured manner and to recommend further sanctions against continuing North Korean violations. Nevertheless, the ROK and the United States should remain open to diplomatic negotiations, making it clear to China and the rest of the international community that the problem is with North Korea. The ROK and the United States have yet to do so.

Operational Control Transition

Some experts believe that U.S. nuclear weapon use in Korea would follow one of several prepared attack options. However, if war ever does occur, any preplanned U.S. nuclear attack options likely would require significant, immediate adjustments based on lessons learned about the North Korean nuclear forces and leadership locations at the beginning of a conflict and the damage done by the North Korean nuclear weapon attacks. Such adjustments would almost certainly require the involvement of the CFC commander. It is difficult to envisage an ROK CFC commander marshaling the U.S. strategic assets for the defense of the peninsula in the way that a U.S. CFC commander would. Unlike in a conventional conflict, in a nuclear conflict, the ROK is not ready to take the principal role in confronting North Korea, especially in the initial stage of a contingency (although the proposed Team of Strategic Advisers might change this situation). This is a key weakness that could lead the North Koreans to interpret the OPCON transition as a sign of faltering U.S. commitment to the defense of the ROK. ROK and U.S. leaders contemplating nuclear warfare in Korea might well conclude that the current command structure between the ROK and the United States should be retained for several more years to ensure the appropriate U.S. nuclear weapon support for the ROK in no ambiguous terms.

Partnership with Japan

The United States has developed its strategy for defeating North Korea based on the assumption that Japan will provide basing access for U.S. forces deploying to Korea and for combat operations against North Korea, especially if there is any serious damage to airfields and other infrastructure in the ROK. Without that access, many U.S. military deployments to Korea would be seriously delayed. To ensure the required access to Japan, the ROK and the United States need to treat Japan more as a partner in the defense of the ROK. North Korea will almost certainly apply major coercion to Japan, potentially including nuclear attacks, in such a scenario, and Japan needs to understand ROK and U.S. strategy because it likely would have to make major sacrifices. It is also important to make sure that if North Korea first seeks to coerce Japan in a conflict, such as by hitting Japan with theater missiles before hitting the ROK, the ROK and the United States are united in supporting and defending Japan, to include retaliation for the attacks on it. Otherwise, Japan could withdraw its assistance to the ROK and the United States.

Information Operations Against North Korea

The leaders of the ROK and the United States have somehow failed to recognize how powerful information operations can be against North Korea. North Korea makes extreme efforts to prevent outside information from reaching its people, fearful that the outside information will undermine Kim's image of power and success and potentially lead to dissent against him because of his many failures. There is no country more ripe for information and influence activities than North Korea and yet so neglected. The ROK and the United States need to unleash their psychological operations forces on the target audiences of the North Korean elite, second-tier leaders, and people.

For example, on his return from the Hanoi Summit with President Trump, Kim claimed a great victory even though that was not the case. The United States should seek to help the North Korean elites recognize that Hanoi was yet another failure of Kim to achieve his promises of gaining sanctions relief. Kim clearly did not know what President Trump was thinking, nor was Kim able to force President Trump to accept the terms that he proposed.

Indeed, North Korea wages unrelenting psychological operations against the United States and the ROK, claiming that they are the eternal enemies of North Korea and blaming the United States for the problems in the North. Kim regularly claims that North Korea needs nuclear weapons to deter U.S. attacks on the North, yet during the decades in which North Korea had no nuclear weapons, the United States never did attack the North. The ROK and U.S. failure to counter North Korea's propaganda confuses people both in the ROK and internationally about the realities of the Korean Peninsula. Significant ROK and U.S. information operations could counter this image and apply serious pressure on North Korea to moderate its nuclear weapons program and other threats.

The United States could discredit the North Korean descriptions of U.S. hostility and demonstrate U.S. magnanimity toward the North Korean people. The ROK needs to prepare a concept of Korean unification that would be advantageous for the North Korean elites; this might even entice some into providing critical regime information to the ROK. This intelligence could facilitate counter-leadership and counterforce attacks on North Korea.

As noted earlier, North Korea wants an agreement to end the Korean War of 1950 to 1953. North Korea has stated repeatedly that the United States needs to end its hostility toward North Korea, which apparently means that such an agreement should end the ROK-U.S. alliance, remove U.S. forces from the ROK, and end the U.S. extended deterrence supporting the ROK.[44] The United States needs to mount an active information operations response, indicating that defending the ROK against North Korean aggression is not a sign of U.S. hostility toward North Korea, but rather a natural result of the Cold War that North Korea has waged since 1953. In fact, the serious hostility

---

[44] Our colleague David Maxwell at the Foundation for Defense of Democracies regularly makes these points.

in the relationship comes from North Korea. The ROK and the United States should argue that the North needs to end its indoctrinations that the United States is the eternal enemy of North Korea—without ending this, there can be no real peace. The onus should be on North Korea to demonstrate an end to hostility.

Working with China

China will oppose most, if not all, of the ROK and U.S. actions that we have proposed to strengthen deterrence of the North Korean nuclear weapon threat. China likely will do this largely because it believes that the United States is a powerful country and that North Korea really does not pose any serious threat against the United States. Rather, China apparently believes that the United States uses the North Korean "threat" to justify its military buildup against China in Northeast Asia. For example, in 2015, when the ROK and the United States contemplated deploying the Terminal High-Altitude Area Defense (THAAD) missile defense system to Korea, China was convinced that the U.S. deployment was really about defending against Chinese ballistic missiles fired at the United States or Japan. China had failed to recognize that the THAAD interceptors, with a range of only 200 km, could not reach the airspace over China.[45] In reality, the only Chinese missiles that THAAD could intercept were ones fired at the ROK, which China eventually recognized. Still, China strongly objected to the U.S. influence on the ROK and justified THAAD-related anti-ROK actions by objecting to the over-the-horizon radar associated with THAAD, despite the fact that China had apparently already deployed similar radars covering the ROK.[46] Angered by the ROK and U.S. action, China implemented a trade war against the ROK that is still ongoing. This war reportedly cost the ROK at least $15.6 billion in 2017 alone,[47] and it forced the Lotte Corporation to abandon $7.2 billion of infrastructure in China.[48]

The ROK and U.S. failure to pursue major information operations on the North Korean nuclear weapon and ballistic missile threats has allowed China to dismiss those threats. The ROK and the United States must now change their strategy and make every effort to get worldwide and especially Chinese recognition of these North Korean threats. The work of the Team of Strategic Advisers described earlier, and its recommendations, should help this effort, making it clear to China that the ROK and

[45]   Bruce Klingner, *South Korea Needs THAAD Missile Defense*, Washington, D.C.: Heritage Foundation, No. 3024, June 12, 2015.

[46]   "Project 2319 Tianbo [Sky Wave]: Over-the-Horizon Backscatter Radar [OTH-B]," GlobalSecurity.org, undated.

[47]   David Josef Volodzko, "China Wins Its War Against South Korea's US THAAD Missile Shield—Without Firing a Shot," *South China Morning Post*, November 18, 2017.

[48]   Kim Da-sol, "Lotte Seeks to Exit China After Investing $7.2b," *Korea Herald*, March 13, 2019.

the United States are serious and are preparing to act in ways that China will not like to counter the North Korean nuclear weapon threat. Although operators trained in psychological operations should be tasked with performing this function, the ROK and the United States should consider broad dissemination of information about the kinds of damage that North Korean nuclear weapons could do to various Chinese cities and other targets and the contexts in which these weapons could be used.[49] China should be reminded that, although North Korea has considered the United States its enemy for seven decades, it has considered China its enemy for many centuries—and still does, despite all that China has done for North Korea.

China does worry that North Korean nuclear weapon actions could drive the United States to take extreme measures against North Korea. China would be furious with a U.S. threat to deploy in the ROK a small number of B61-12 bombs, and the required aircraft for their delivery, if North Korea crosses a U.S.-designated threshold of North Korean nuclear weapon inventory, because this action would significantly increase the risk of accidental nuclear war in the theater. Well before North Korea reaches this threshold, the United States needs to begin making this threat, hoping to get China to pressure North Korea to accept a nuclear weapon production freeze. If North Korea exceeds the nuclear weapon inventory threshold for B61-12 deployment, the United States should explain to China that if North Korea freezes its nuclear weapon production and reduces its nuclear weapon inventory to the threshold, the B61-12s and associated aircraft will be withdrawn from the ROK; the North must make a choice.

Finally, China appears to believe that if North Korea is treated appropriately and with patience, it will become a responsible member of the Northeast Asia community and responsive to Chinese influence. This would be consistent with Chinese leader Xi Jinping's stated intent for China to become the global hegemon by 2049.[50] However, North Korea is fiercely independent of Chinese influence: "Pyongyang has never cared about Beijing's concerns."[51] For example, although China reportedly told Kim Jong-un not to hurt his older half-brother, Kim had his brother killed in Malaysia with a banned nerve agent.[52] China apparently was sensitive about that action, suspending

---

[49] A survey of Chinese writings on North Korean nuclear weapons, covering 2012 to 2019, concluded "that Pyongyang's nuclear program not only threatens China's national security and interests but also allows the United States to strengthen the South Korea–U.S. alliance and implement strategic deterrence against Beijing" (Haofan Fang, "Sino–DPRK Relations and Chinese Perception Toward North Korea's Nuclear Issue: Meta-Analysis on Chinese Literature Since 2012," *Korean Journal of Defense Analysis*, Vol. 32, No. 4, December 2020, p. 625). So, there appears to be some existing Chinese concern for China's security.

[50] Brands, 2020.

[51] Andrei Lankov and Peter Ward, "No, You're the Puppet: Why North Korea Isn't a Chinese Satellite," NK News, May 14, 2020.

[52] Simon Denyer, "China Suspends North Korean Coal Imports, Striking at Regime's Financial Lifeline," *Washington Post*, February 18, 2017.

coal imports from North Korea—a major source of the North's hard currency—just five days after the murder. Unfortunately for China, North Korea is more likely to become even more self-assertive and aggressive, especially as it builds more nuclear weapons. An assertive North Korea will almost certainly set a bad example for other countries, encouraging them to defy Chinese influence and to build nuclear weapons to sustain their independence. In short, North Korea is not, in reality, China's friend and needs to be reined in for Chinese purposes as much as for U.S. purposes.

References

"2013 Plenary Meeting of WPK Central Committee and 7th Session of Supreme People's Assembly," North Korean Economy Watch, April 1, 2013. As of February 16, 2021:
https://www.nkeconwatch.com/2013/04/01/
2013-plenary-meeting-of-wpk-central-committee-and-supreme-peoples-assembly/

Acton, James M., Jeffrey Lewis, and David Wright, "Video Analysis of the Reentry of North Korea's July 28, 2017 Missile Test," Carnegie Endowment for International Peace, November 9, 2018. As of February 17, 2021:
https://carnegieendowment.org/2018/11/09/
video-analysis-of-reentry-of-north-korea-s-july-28-2017-missile-test-pub-78269

Akulov, Andrei, "South Korea Forms Special Unit to Kill North Korean Leader," Strategic Culture Foundation, January 18, 2017. As of February 17, 2021:
https://www.strategic-culture.org/news/2017/01/18/
south-korea-forms-special-unit-kill-north-korean-leader/

Albert, Eleanor, "North Korea's Military Capabilities," Council on Foreign Relations, September 5, 2017.

Albright, David, *Future Directions in the DPRK's Nuclear Weapons Program: Three Scenarios for 2020*, Washington, D.C.: US-Korea Institute at SAIS, 2015.

——— , "North Korea's Nuclear Capabilities: A Fresh Look," presentation slides, Washington, D.C.: Institute for Science and International Security, April 22, 2017. As of February 17, 2021:
https://isis-online.org/uploads/isis-reports/documents/North_Korea_Talk_April_28_2017_Final.pdf

Albright, David, and Robert Avagyan, *Recent Doubling of Floor Space at North Korean Gas Centrifuge Plant: Is North Korea Doubling Its Enrichment Capacity at Yongbyon?* Washington, D.C.: Institute for Science and International Security Imagery Brief, August 7, 2013.

Albright, David, and Christina Walrond, *North Korea's Estimated Stocks of Plutonium and Weapon-Grade Uranium*, Washington, D.C.: Institute for Science and International Security, August 16, 2012. As of February 17, 2021:
https://isis-online.org/uploads/isis-reports/documents/
dprk_fissile_material_production_16Aug2012.pdf

Allard, Léonie, Mathieu Duchâtel, and François Godement, "Pre-Empting Defeat: In Search of North Korea's Nuclear Doctrine," London, United Kingdom: European Council on Foreign Relations, ECFR/237, 2017. As of February 18, 2021:
http://www.ecfr.eu/publications/summary/
pre_empting_defeat_in_search_of_north_koreas_nuclear_doctrine

Allison, Graham T., Jr., "North Korea's Lesson: Nukes for Sale," *New York Times*, February 12, 2013.

Baek, Jieun, "Why Foreign Information in North Korea Is Such a Big Deal," NK News, October 19, 2016.

Bae Sung-won, "김정은 '미북회담 목적은 핵보유국 인정' ···하노이 회담 앞서 군부에 핵개 발 지침 [Kim Jong Un 'The Goal of the U.S.-North Korean Summit Was to Be Recognized as an Official Nuclear State' . . . Military Nuclear Development Guidelines Ahead of the Hanoi Summit]," Voice of America, June 18, 2019. As of March 2, 2021: https://www.voakorea.com/korea/korea-politics/4961300

Baik Sung-won, "Leaked N. Korean Document Shows Internal Policy Against Denuclearization," Voice of America, June 17, 2019a.

———, "Experts: Step-by-Step Approach Needed in Denuclearization Deal with North Korea," Voice of America, June 25, 2019b.

Barrie, Douglas, and Joseph Dempsey, "What North Korea's Latest Missile Parade Tells Us, and What It Doesn't," International Institute for Strategic Studies, October 12, 2020. As of February 17, 2021: https://www.iiss.org/blogs/analysis/2020/10/north-korea-missile-parade

Bechtol, Bruce E., Jr., *North Korean Military Proliferation in the Middle East and Africa: Enabling Violence and Instability*, Lexington, Ky.: University Press of Kentucky, 2018.

———, "North Korea, China, and Iran: The Axis of Missiles?" *National Interest*, October 25, 2020.

Bennett, Bruce W., "Stability in Northeast Asia and the North Korean 'Christmas Present,'" *RAND Blog*, December 24, 2019. As of February 17, 2021: https://www.rand.org/blog/2019/12/stability-in-northeast-asia-and-the-north-korean-christmas.html

Bennett, Dashiell, "North Korea Is Now Threatening a Preemptive Nuclear Attack," *The Atlantic*, March 7, 2013.

Bermudez, Joseph S., Jr., "New Hovercraft Base at Sasŭlp'o," *KPA Journal*, Vol. 2, No. 2, February 2011, pp. 1–10.

———, "Sil-li Ballistic Missile Support Facility," Beyond Parallel, Center for Strategic and International Studies, May 5, 2020. As of February 17, 2021: https://beyondparallel.csis.org/sil-li-ballistic-missile-support-facility/

Biden, Joe, "Hope for Our Better Future," Yonhap News Agency, October 29, 2020.

Bistline, John E., David M. Blum, Chris Rinaldi, Gabriel Shields-Estrada, Siegfried S. Hecker, and M. Elisabeth Paté-Cornell, "A Bayesian Model to Assess the Size of North Korea's Uranium Enrichment Program," *Science & Global Security*, Vol. 23, No. 2, 2015, pp. 71–100.

Brands, Hal, "What Does China Really Want? To Dominate the World," *Japan Times*, May 22, 2020.

Brumfiel, Geoff, "North Korea's Newest Missile Appears Similar to Advanced Russian Design," NPR, May 8, 2019.

Bureau of Intelligence and Research, "The Secretary's Morning Intelligence Summary," U.S. Department of State, March 29, 1994. As of February 17, 2021: https://nsarchive2.gwu.edu/NSAEBB/NSAEBB421/docs/19940329.pdf

Carlin, Robert, and Robert Jervis, *Nuclear North Korea: How Will It Behave?* Washington, D.C.: US-Korea Institute at SAIS, October 2015. As of February 18, 2021: https://www.38north.org/wp-content/uploads/2015/10/CarlinJervis-final.pdf

Cheng Xiaohe, "The Evolution of Sino-North Korean Relations in the 1960s," *Asian Perspective*, Vol. 34, No. 2, 2010, pp. 173–199.

Choe Sang-Hun, "North Korea Threatens to Attack U.S. with 'Lighter and Smaller Nukes,'" *New York Times*, March 5, 2013a.

———, "N. Korea Threatens to Attak S. Korean Presidential Office," *Dong-A Ilbo*, November 23, 2013b. As of February 17, 2021:
http://english.donga.com/srv/service.php3?bicode=050000&biid=2013112374388

———, "North Korea Unveils What Appears to Be New ICBM During Military Parade," *New York Times*, last updated January 13, 2021a.

———, "Kim Jong-un Vows to Boost North Korea's Nuclear Capability as Leverage with Biden," *New York Times*, last updated January 15, 2021b.

Choi Ha-young and John G. Grisafi, "North Korea's Nuclear Force Reshuffles Its Politics, Economy," NK News, February 11, 2016.

Choi Hyun-jung, "Kim Jong-il 'Acquired the Status of Nuclear Power in 2012,'" *Dong A Ilbo*, May 11, 2009. As of February 17, 2021:
https://www.donga.com/news/Politics/article/all/20090511/8730463/9

Choi Kang, "Concerned About the Korean Version of 'Stockholm Syndrome,'" *Chosun Ilbo*, January 19, 2021. As of February 17, 2021:
https://www.chosun.com/opinion/chosun_column/2021/01/19/
YRRGBFG4WJEYFIZHOTOAZGOLPY/

Choi Kang and Kim Gibum, "A Thought on North Korea's Nuclear Doctrine," *Korean Journal of Defense Analysis*, Vol. 29, No. 4, December 2017, pp. 495–511. As of February 25, 2021:
https://kida.re.kr/cmm/viewBoardImageFile.do?idx=23651

Choi Soo-hyang, "Kim Calls U.S. 'Principal Enemy,' Vows to Continue Nuclear Development," Yonhap News Agency, January 9, 2021.

Chung Kyung-young, "Realitics and Strategies in Managing North Korea's Nuclear Challenge," *China Quarterly of International Strategic Studies*, Vol. 2, No. 4, 2016, pp. 465–484.

Chung, Minn, "Seoul Will Become a Sea of Fire . . . ," *Bulletin of Concerned Asian Scholars*, Vol. 26, No. 1–2, 1994, pp. 132–135.

Chung Won-shik, Republic of Korea, and Yon Hyong-muk, Democratic People's Republic of Korea, Joint Declaration of the Denuclearization of the Korean Peninsula, January 20, 1992. As of February 18, 2021:
https://peacemaker.un.org/sites/peacemaker.un.org/files/
KR%20KP_920120_JointDeclarationDenuclearizationKoreanPeninsula.pdf

Chun, In-Bum, "The Future of the UN Command," 38 North, September 12, 2017. As of February 17, 2021:
https://www.38north.org/2017/09/ibchun091217/

Clapper, James, "Ending the Dead End in North Korea," *New York Times*, May 19, 2018.

Coats, Daniel R., Director of National Intelligence, "Worldwide Threat Assessment of the US Intelligence Community," statement presented before the U.S. Senate Select Committee on Intelligence on January 29, 2019, Washington, D.C.: Office of the Director of National Intelligence, 2019. As of February 17, 2021:
https://www.dni.gov/files/ODNI/documents/2019-ATA-SFR---SSCI.pdf

David, Jack, "Address: If You Want Peace, Prepare for War—U.S. Military Pre-Eminence and Why It Matters," Hudson Institute, March 8, 2014. As of February 18, 2021:
https://www.hudson.org/research/
10155-address-if-you-want-peace-prepare-for-war-u-s-military-pre-eminence-and-why-it-matters

Denyer, Simon, "China Suspends North Korean Coal Imports, Striking at Regime's Financial Lifeline," *Washington Post*, February 18, 2017.

Dong-Ki Sung, "North Korea Announces It Has No Intention of Developing Nuke Weapons," *Dong-A Ilbo*, January 22, 2003. As of February 17, 2021:
https://www.donga.com/en/article/all/20030122/226952/1/
North-Korea-Announces-It-Has-No-Intention-of-Developing-Nuke-Weapons

Dr. Strangelove, dir. Stanley Kubrick, Columbia Pictures, 1964.

Eberstadt, Nicholas, "A Skeptical View," *Wall Street Journal*, September 21, 2005.

"[Editorial] S. Korea-US Joint Exercises Need to Be Delayed to Enable Bold Change in Inter-Korean Dialogue," *Hankyoreh*, July 22, 2020. As of February 18, 2021:
http://www.hani.co.kr/arti/english_edition/e_editorial/954774.html

Elleman, Michael, "The New Hwasong-15 ICBM: A Significant Improvement That May Be Ready as Early as 2018," 38 North, November 30, 2017. As of February 18, 2021:
https://www.38north.org/2017/11/melleman113017/

Fang, Haofan, "Sino–DPRK Relations and Chinese Perception Toward North Korea's Nuclear Issue: Meta-Analysis on Chinese Literature Since 2012," *Korean Journal of Defense Analysis*, Vol. 32, No. 4, December 2020, pp. 625–653.

Federation of American Scientists, "Yongbyon [Nyongbyon] N39º48' E125º48'," webpage, last updated March 4, 2000. As of February 17, 2021:
https://fas.org/nuke/guide/dprk/facility/yongbyon.htm

Fifield, Anna, "In Drills, U.S., South Korea Practice Striking North's Nuclear Plants, Leaders," *Washington Post*, March 7, 2016a.

———, "North Korea's Making a Lot of Threats These Days. How Worried Should We Be?" *Washington Post*, March 10, 2016b.

———, "North Korea's Definition of 'Denuclearization' Is Very Different from Trump's," *Washington Post*, April 9, 2018.

Financial Crimes Enforcement Network, "Advisory on North Korea's Use of the International Financial System," FIN-2017-A007, U.S. Department of the Treasury, November 2, 2017. As of February 16, 2021:
https://www.fincen.gov/sites/default/files/advisory/2017-11-02/
DPRK%20Financing%20Advisory%20FINAL%2011022017.pdf

Fisher, Max, "Here's North Korea's Official Declaration of 'War,'" *Washington Post*, March 29, 2013.

Fitzpatrick, Mark, *North Korean Proliferation Challenges: The Role of the European Union*, Stockholm, Sweden: Stockholm International Peace Research Institute, Non-Proliferation Paper No. 18, June 2012. As of February 18, 2021:
http://www.sipri.org/research/disarmament/eu-consortium/publications/nonproliferation-paper-18

Freier, Nathan, John Schaus, and William Braun, *An Army Transformed: USINDOPACOM Hypercompetition and US Army Theater Design*, Carlisle, Pa.: Strategic Studies Institute and US Army War College Press, 2020.

"김정일 유서 전문 [Full Text of Kim Jong-il's Will]," U Korea News, November 23, 2012. As of February 17, 2021:
http://www.ukoreanews.com/news/articleView.html?idxno=657

Gentile, Gian, Yvonne K. Crane, Dan Madden, Timothy M. Bonds, Bruce W. Bennett, Michael J. Mazarr, and Andrew Scobell, *Four Problems on the Korean Peninsula: North Korea's Expanding Nuclear Capabilities Drive a Complex Set of Problems*, Santa Monica, Calif.: RAND Corporation, TL-271-A, 2019. As of February 18, 2021:
https://www.rand.org/pubs/tools/TL271.html

Gertz, Bill, "Report: N. Korea Has Nuclear Warheads for Missiles," *Washington Free Beacon*, May 5, 2014.

Grover, John Dale, "Engagement First: Why Some Koreans See Peacemaking and Peacebuilding as the Solution to North Korea," *National Interest*, May 11, 2020.

Ha, Mathew, "Amended North Korean Constitution Reaffirms Kim Jong Un's Steadfast Faith in His Nuclear Arsenal," Foundation for Defense of Democracies, July 15, 2019. As of February 18, 2021:
https://www.fdd.org/analysis/2019/07/15/amended-north-korean-constitution-reaffirms-kim-jong-uns-steadfast-faith-in-his-nuclear-arsenal/

Haggard, Stephan, "Nuclear Doctrine: What the North Koreans Are Actually Saying," Peterson Institute for International Economics, August 16, 2017. As of February 19, 2021:
https://www.piie.com/blogs/north-korea-witness-transformation/nuclear-doctrine-what-north-koreans-are-actually-saying

Haggard, Stephan, and Tai Ming Cheung, *North Korea's Nuclear and Missile Programs*, San Diego, Calif.: UC Institute on Global Conflict and Cooperation, IGCC Policy Brief, July 2020.

Hamedy, Saba, "President Trump Showed Kim Jong Un This Hollywood-Style Video to Pitch Him on Peace," CNN, June 12, 2018.

Hansen, Nick, Robert Kelley, and Allison Puccioni, "North Korean Nuclear Programme Advances," *Janes*, March 30, 2016.

Harris, Bryan, "North Korea Threatens Nuclear Destruction of Japan," *Financial Times*, September 14, 2017.

Hecker, Siegfried S., *A Return Trip to North Korea's Yongbyon Nuclear Complex*, Nautilus Institute for Security and Sustainability, NAPSNet Special Reports, November 22, 2010. As of February 19, 2021:
https://nautilus.org/napsnet/napsnet-special-reports/a-return-trip-to-north-koreas-yongbyon-nuclear-complex/

———, *Can the North Korean Nuclear Crisis Be Resolved?* Stanford, Calif.: Center for International Security and Cooperation, Stanford University, March 21, 2012. As of February 19, 2021:
https://cisac.fsi.stanford.edu/publications/can_north_korea_nuclear_crisis_be_resolved

Hecker, Siegfried S., Chaim Braun, and Chris Lawrence, "North Korea's Stockpiles of Fissile Material," *Korea Observer*, Vol. 47, No. 4, Winter 2016, pp. 721–749.

Hecker, Siegfried S., and Robert L. Carlin, "We Are Teetering on the Edge of a Hinge Point with North Korea," Berggruen Institute, August 5, 2019.

Hulina, Jake, "Nothing If Not Persistent: North Korean Exploitation of Fijian and Cambodian Flags at Sea," *Arms Control Wonk*, blog, August 11, 2020. As of February 18, 2021:
https://www.armscontrolwonk.com/archive/1209892/nothing-if-not-persistent-north-korean-exploitation-of-fijian-and-cambodian-flags-at-sea/

Hyten, John E., "Missile Defense and Defeat: A Conversation with the Vice Chairman," transcript of webinar on February 23, 2021, Center for Strategic and International Studies, 2021. As of March 2, 2021:
https://www.csis.org/events/missile-defense-and-defeat-conversation-vice-chairman

International Crisis Group, *The Korean Peninsula Crisis (II): From Fire and Fury to Freeze-for-Freeze*, Brussels, Belgium, Asia Report No. 294, January 23, 2018. As of February 17, 2021: https://www.crisisgroup.org/asia/north-east-asia/korean-peninsula/294-korean-peninsula-crisis-ii-fire-and-fury-freeze-freeze

"Iranian Nuke Chief Was in N. Korea for Atomic Test," *Times of Israel*, February 17, 2013.

Jackson, Van, "Preventing Nuclear War with North Korea: What to Do After the Test," *Foreign Affairs*, September 11, 2016.

Jeong Yong-soo, "Kim Jong-il's Final Orders: Build More Weapons," *JoongAng Daily*, January 29, 2013.

Jeong Yong-Soo, Baek Min-Jeong, and Shim Kyu-Seok, "Secret Enrichment Plant Is Right Next to Yongbyon: Sources," *JoongAng Daily*, March 5, 2019.

Jeong Yong-soo and Ser Myo-ja, "Kim Jong-un Ordered a Plan for a 7-Day Asymmetric War: Officials," *JoongAng Daily*, January 7, 2015.

———, "North Shrank Its Nukes Pre-2014," *JoongAng Daily*, August 11, 2017.

jin0619@donga.com, "NK Has Built Uranium Enrichment Facilities," *Dong-A Ilbo*, February 18, 2009. As of February 18, 2021: http://www.donga.com/en/article/all/20090218/261399/

Johnson, Jesse, "NHK Video Casts Doubt on North Korean ICBM Re-Entry Capabilities and Effectiveness," *Japan Times*, August 1, 2017.

Jo Sang-jin, "미 전문가들 "북한의 군축협상 시도 일축해야 [U.S. Experts Say, "North Korea's Military Disarmament Attempt Should Be Dismissed]," Voice of America, October 5, 2019. As of February 25, 2021: https://www.voakorea.com/korea/korea-politics/5109659

julesyi@yna.co.kr, "New Satellite Images Show N. Korea's Hidden Submarine Capable of Firing Ballistic Missiles," Yonhap News Agency, January 6, 2020.

Jung In-hwan, "Is N. Korea Raising Peninsula Tensions in Bid for US Negotiations?" *Hankyoreh*, August 11, 2017. As of February 18, 2021: http://english.hani.co.kr/arti/english_edition/e_northkorea/806473.html

Kang Jin-kyu and Kang Chan-su, "North Korea's Fifth Nuclear Test Strongest Yet," *JoongAng Daily*, September 9, 2016.

Keating, Joshua, "Kim and Trump Don't Mean the Same Thing When They Talk About 'Denuclearization,'" *Slate*, March 28, 2018.

Kerry, John F., "Breaking the Cycle of North Korean Provocations," opening statement presented before the U.S. Senate Committee on Foreign Relations on March 1, 2011, Washington, D.C.: U.S. Government Printing Office, 2011, pp. 1–4. As of February 18, 2021: https://www.foreign.senate.gov/imo/media/doc/030111_Transcript_Breaking%20The%20Cycle%20of%20North%20Korean%20Provocations.pdf

Kim, Christine, and Soyoung Kim, "North Korea Says Seriously Considering Plan to Strike Guam: KCNA," Yahoo News, August 8, 2017.

Kim Dang, "단독] 대북 차관 1조617억원···北, 한푼도 안갚아 [Exclusive: Vice Minister of North Korea Did Not Pay Back Any of the 1 Trillion 61.7 Billion KRW in Loans to North Korea]," UPI News, June 19, 2020. As of February 25, 2021: https://www.upinews.kr/newsView/upi202006190071

Kim Da-sol, "Lotte Seeks to Exit China After Investing $7.2b," *Korea Herald*, March 13, 2019.

Kim Dong-hyun, "미 전문가들, 주한미군 관련 육군대학원 보고서에 엇갈린 반응 [U.S. Experts: Report from the Army War College Provided Conflicting Perspectives on USFK]," Voice of America, July 31, 2020. As of February 25, 2021:
https://www.voakorea.com/korea/korea-politics/usfk-review

Kim, Duyeon, "Washington and Seoul Must Heal Their Alliance: Confronting North Korean and Chinese Aggression Requires It," *Foreign Affairs*, January 26, 2021. As of February 25, 2021:
https://www.foreignaffairs.com/articles/united-states/2021-01-26/washington-and-seoul-must-heal-their-alliance

Kim, Hyung-jin, "North Korea Says Underwater-Launched Missile Test Succeeded," Associated Press, October 3, 2019.

Kim Hyun Sik, "The Secret History of Kim Jong Il," *Foreign Policy*, October 6, 2009.

Kim, J. James, Kim Chong Woo, Kim Seonkyung, and Ham Geon Hee, *Assessing South Korea's Civil Defense Emergency Evacuation Facilities*, Seoul, South Korea: Asan Institute for Policy Studies, April 3, 2018. As of February 18, 2021:
http://en.asaninst.org/contents/assessing-south-koreas-civil-defense-emergency-evacuation-facilities/

Kim, Jack, "North Korea Says Missile Test Simulated Attack on South's Airfields," Reuters, July 19, 2016.

Kim Jeong Hun, "Kim Il Sung University Graduates Ordered into Doctoral Programs," Daily NK, December 23, 2019.

Kim, Jeongmin, "Apologies, Tears and a 'War Deterrent': Top Quotes from Kim Jong Un's Speech," NK News, October 12, 2020.

Kim, Jeongmin, and Kelly Kasulis, "South Korea Revokes Corporate License for Two Defector-Led Activist Groups," NK News, July 17, 2020.

Kim Jong-un, "New Year Address of Supreme Leader Kim Jong Un for 2019," trans. *Rodong Sinmun*, National Committee on North Korea, January 1, 2019. As of February 17, 2021:
https://www.ncnk.org/resources/publications/kimjongun_2019_newyearaddress.pdf/file_view

"Kim Jong Un Observes and Guides Ballistic Missile Drill," North Korea Leadership Watch, July 19, 2016. As of February 16, 2021:
https://nkleadershipwatch.wordpress.com/2016/07/19/kim-jong-un-observes-and-guides-ballistic-missile-drill/

"Kim Jong Un Observes and Guides Mobile Ballistic Missile Drill and Watches KPA Tank Competition," North Korea Leadership Watch, March 10, 2016. As of February 16, 2021:
https://nkleadershipwatch.wordpress.com/2016/03/10/kim-jong-un-observes-and-guides-mobile-ballistic-drill-and-watches-kpa-tank-competition/

"Kim Jong Un Supervises Missile Drill," North Korea Leadership Watch, March 6, 2017. As of February 16, 2021:
https://nkleadershipwatch.wordpress.com/2017/03/06/kim-jong-un-supervises-missile-drill/

Kim Myong Chol, "Farewell to 1994 Agreed Framework!" Northeast Asia Peace and Security Network Policy Forum Online, November 24, 1998. As of February 18, 2021:
https://web.archive.org/web/20000817005713/http://www.nautilus.org/fora/security/23C_Kim.html

Kim Sang-hyup, "South Korea and the United States Build Precision Strikes in the 5th Stage of North Korean Anti-Missiles," *Munhwa Ilbo*, October 10, 2012. As of February 18, 2021:
http://www.munhwa.com/news/view.html?no=2012101001070123029002

Kim, Sarah, "Trump Tells Fox About 5 Nuclear Sites in North," *JoongAng Daily*, May 21, 2019.

Kim Tong-Hyung, "Moon Urges Biden to Learn from Trump's N. Korea Diplomacy," Associated Press, January 18, 2020.

Kim, Yongho, "North Korea's Use of Terror and Coercive Diplomacy: Looking for Their Circumstantial Variants," *Korean Journal of Defense Analysis*, Vol. 14, No. 1, 2002, pp. 45–67.

Klingner, Bruce, *South Korea Needs THAAD Missile Defense*, Washington, D.C.: Heritage Foundation, No. 3024, June 12, 2015. As of February 17, 2021:
https://www.heritage.org/defense/report/south-korea-needs-thaad-missile-defense

Klug, Foster, and Kim Tong-Hyung, "Rhetoric or Real? N. Korea Nuclear Test May Be a Bit of Both," Associated Press, September 10, 2016.

Korea Immigration Service, *2019 Statistical Yearbook of Immigration and Foreigners Policy*, July 13, 2020. As of February 18, 2021:
https://www.immigration.go.kr/immigration/1570/subview.do

"KPA Supreme Command Issues Statement," North Korea Leadership Watch, February 23, 2016. As of February 16, 2021:
https://nkleadershipwatch.wordpress.com/2016/02/23/kpa-supreme-command-issues-statement-2/

Krepon, Michael, and Chris Gagne, eds., *The Stability-Instability Paradox: Nuclear Weapons and Brinksmanship in South Asia*, Washington, D.C.: Stimson, No. 38, June 2001. As of February 18, 2021:
https://www.stimson.org/2001/
stability-instability-paradox-nuclear-weapons-and-brinksmanship-south-asia/

Kristensen, Hans M., and Matthew McKinzie, "Video Shows Earth-Penetrating Capability of B61-12 Nuclear Bomb," Federation of American Scientists, January 14, 2016. As of February 18, 2021:
https://fas.org/blogs/security/2016/01/b61-12_earth-penetration/

Kristensen, Hans M., and Robert S. Norris, "A History of US Nuclear Weapons in South Korea," *Bulletin of the Atomic Scientists*, Vol. 73, No. 6, 2017, pp. 349–357.

Kube, Courtney, Ken Dilanian, and Carol E. Lee, "North Korea Has Increased Nuclear Production at Secret Sites, Say U.S. Officials," NBC News, last updated June 30, 2018.

Lankov, Andrei, and Wang Son-taek, "Is the Dream of Korean Reunification Dead?" NK News Podcast Ep. 162, December 24, 2020. As of February 17, 2021:
https://www.nknews.org/category/north-korea-news-podcast/latest/
is-the-dream-of-korean-reunification-dead-nknews-podcast-ep-162/896421/

Lankov, Andrei, and Peter Ward, "No, You're the Puppet: Why North Korea Isn't a Chinese Satellite," NK News, May 14, 2020.

"Law on Consolidating Position of Nuclear Weapons State Adopted," KCNA Watch, January 4, 2013. As of February 16, 2021:
https://kcnawatch.org/newstream/1451896124-739013370/law-on-consolidating-position-of-/

Lee Jung-eun, "통일비용, 천문학적이라고?···전문가들 "분단비용 고려해야 [Unification Costs Are Astronomical? Experts Say Division of Costs Should Be Considered]," *Hankook-ilbo*, May 2, 2018. As of February 25, 2021:
https://www.hankookilbo.com/News/Read/201805021274628429

Leitenberg, Milton, *Studies of Military R&D and Weapons Development*, Center for International and Security Studies, University of Maryland, 1984. As of March 2, 2021:
https://fas.org/man/eprint/leitenberg/

Levy, Jack S., "The Diversionary Theory of War: A Critique," in Manus I. Midlarsky, ed., *Handbook of War Studies*, Boston, Mass.: Unwin Hyman, 1989, pp. 259–288.

Lewis, Jeffrey, "North Korean Targeting," *Arms Control Wonk*, blog, April 8, 2013. As of February 18, 2021:
https://www.armscontrolwonk.com/archive/206515/north-korean-targeting/

———, "North Korea's Nuclear Weapons: The Great Miniaturization Debate," 38 North, February 5, 2015a. As of February 18, 2021:
http://38north.org/2015/02/jlewis020515/

———, "Revisiting the Agreed Framework," 38 North, May 15, 2015b. As of February 18, 2021:
https://www.38north.org/2015/05/jlewis051415/

Malus, Katherine, and Hilary Huaici, "How North Korea Got a Seat at the Nuclear Table," Center for Nuclear Studies, July 13, 2018. As of February 18, 2021:
https://k1project.columbia.edu/content/how-north-korea-got-seat-nuclear-table

Manyin, Mark E., *North Korea–Japan Relations: The Normalization Talks and the Compensation/ Reparations Issue*, Washington, D.C.: Congressional Research Service, Library of Congress, RS20526, 2002. As of February 18, 2021:
https://digital.library.unt.edu/ark:/67531/metacrs3109/

Military-Today.com, "Iskander," webpage, undated. As of February 16, 2021:
http://www.military-today.com/missiles/iskander.htm

Ministry of Defense of Japan, "Korean Peninsula," in *Defense of Japan 2014*, Tokyo, Japan, 2014, pp. 15–31. As of February 25, 2021:
https://warp.da.ndl.go.jp/info:ndljp/pid/11591426/www.mod.go.jp/e/publ/w_paper/pdf/2014/DOJ2014_1-1-2_web_1031.pdf

Ministry of Unification of South Korea, "Korea Institute for National Unification Dictionary," webpage, December 31, 2016. As of February 18, 2021:
https://www.uniedu.go.kr/uniedu/home/brd/bbsatcl/nknow/view.do?id=31957&mid=SM00000536&limit=10&eqViewYn=true

Missile Defense Advocacy Alliance, "North Korea," webpage, March 2019. As of February 23, 2021:
https://missiledefenseadvocacy.org/missile-threat-and-proliferation/todays-missile-threat/north-korea/

Missile Defense Project, "Missiles of North Korea," webpage, *Missile Threat*, Center for Strategic and International Studies, last updated November 30, 2020. As of February 23, 2021:
https://missilethreat.csis.org/country/dprk/

Mitchell, Ellen, "Pentagon Chief Says US Looking to Put Intermediate-Range Missiles in Asia," *The Hill*, August 3, 2019.

Moon Jae-in and Kim Jong-un, Panmunjom Declaration on Peace, Prosperity and Reunification of the Korean Peninsula, Panmunjom, South Korea, April 27, 2018. As of February 18, 2021:
http://english1.president.go.kr/BriefingSpeeches/Speeches/32

Moon Kwan-hyun, "北통신 '핵무력, 동족 겨냥 아니다…철저히 미국 겨냥 [Nuclear Forces Are Not Targeted Toward Their Own People, It Is Surely for the United States]," Yonhap News Agency, February 24, 2018. As of February 25, 2021:
https://www.yna.co.kr/view/AKR20180224054300014

Moon Sung-hwi, "North Korea Moves Its Wartime Command Center to Nampo Taesan," *Liberty Korea Post*, July 7, 2018. As of February 18, 2021:
http://www.lkp.news/news/article.html?no=4808

Morris, Lyle J., Michael J. Mazarr, Jeffrey W. Hornung, Stephanie Pezard, Anika Binnendijk, and Marta Kepe, *Gaining Competitive Advantage in the Gray Zone: Response Options for Coercive Aggression Below the Threshold of Major War*, Santa Monica, Calif.: RAND Corporation, RR-2942-OSD, 2019. As of February 18, 2021:
https://www.rand.org/pubs/research_reports/RR2942.html

Mount, Adam, *Conventional Deterrence of North Korea*, Washington, D.C.: Federation of American Scientists, 2019. As of February 17, 2021:
https://fas.org/wp-content/uploads/2019/12/FAS-CDNK.pdf

Mugford, William, and Jack Liu, "North Korea's Yongbyon Nuclear Facility: New Activity at the Plutonium Production Complex," 38 North, September 8, 2015. As of February 16, 2021:
http://38north.org/2015/09/yongbyon090815/

Mullen, Mike, Sam Nunn, and Adam Mount, *A Sharper Choice on North Korea: Engaging China for a Stable Northeast Asia*, New York: Council on Foreign Relations, Independent Task Force Report No. 74, 2016. As of February 18, 2021:
https://cdn.cfr.org/sites/default/files/pdf/2016/09/TFR74_North%20Korea.pdf

"N. Korea Calls Itself 'Nuclear-Armed State' in Revised Constitution," Yonhap News Agency, May 30, 2012. As of February 18, 2021:
https://en.yna.co.kr/view/AEN20120530005200315

"N. Korea Digging New Tunnel at Its Nuke Test Site: Official," Yonhap News Agency, October 30, 2015.

"N. Korean FM Claims U.S. Nuclear Threats Result in Pyongyang's Nuclear Development," *Korea Times*, April 21, 2016.

"N.Korea Puts Nuclear Arms in Constitution," *Chosun Ilbo*, May 31, 2012. As of February 16, 2021:
http://english.chosun.com/site/data/html_dir/2012/05/31/2012053100646.html

"N.Korea Resumes Tests for Smaller Missile Warheads," *Chosun Ilbo*, February 26, 2015. As of February 15, 2021:
http://english.chosun.com/site/data/html_dir/2015/02/26/2015022601825.html

"N. Korea Says No Plans to Give Up Nuclear Capabilities," Yonhap News Agency, May 28, 2013.

"N. Korea Threatens to Turn Japan into 'Nuclear Sea of Flames,'" Yonhap News Agency, September 29, 2004. As of February 24, 2021:
https://en.yna.co.kr/view/AEN20040929000200325

"N. Korea Warns of 'Precision Strike' on U.S. Bases," CBS News, April 5, 2013.

Nakashima, Ellen, and Joby Warrick, "North Korea Working to Conceal Key Aspects of Its Nuclear Program, U.S. Officials Say," *Washington Post*, June 30, 2018.

Narang, Vipin, *Nuclear Strategy in the Modern Era: Regional Powers and International Conflict*, Princeton, N.J.: Princeton University Press, 2014.

"National Defense Commission, Foreign Ministry Issues Statements on Foal Eagle, Key Resolve," North Korea Leadership Watch, March 6, 2016. As of February 16, 2021:
https://nkleadershipwatch.wordpress.com/2016/03/06/
national-defense-commission-foreign-ministry-issues-statements-on-foal-eagle-key-resolve/

National Research Council, *Effects of Nuclear Earth-Penetrator and Other Weapons*, Washington, D.C.: The National Academies Press, 2005.

Neely, Bill, "North Korea Warns It Would Use Nuclear Weapons First If Threatened," NBC News, October 16, 2016.

Niksch, Larry A., *North Korea's Nuclear Weapons Development and Diplomacy*, Washington, D.C.: Congressional Research Service, RL33590, January 5, 2010. As of February 18, 2021: https://fas.org/sgp/crs/nuke/RL33590.pdf

NK News, "North Korea Military Parade 2020—Livestream & Analysis," video, YouTube, October 10, 2020. As of February 17, 2021: https://www.youtube.com/watch?v=w8dZl9f3faY&t=6740s

Noh Ji-won, "Defense Ministry Changes Terminology for 'Three-Axis System' of Military Response," *Hankyoreh*, January 13, 2019. As of February 18, 2021: http://english.hani.co.kr/arti/english_edition/e_national/878208.html

"North Korean Missile Proliferation," hearing before the Subcommittee on International Security, Proliferation, and Federal Services of the Committee on Governmental Affairs, U.S. Senate on October 21, 1997, Washington, D.C.: U.S. Government Printing Office, 1997. As of February 16, 2021: www.gpo.gov/fdsys/pkg/CHRG-105shrg44649/pdf/CHRG-105shrg44649.pdf

"North Korean Nuclear Weapons," CIA estimate for Congress, November 19, 2002. As of February 16, 2021: http://www.fas.org/nuke/guide/dprk/nuke/cia111902.html

"North Korea Pledges Not to Abandon Nukes," AsiaOne, February 21, 2010. As of February 16, 2021: https://www.asiaone.com/News/Latest%2BNews/Asia/Story/A1Story20100221-199951.html

"North Korea Ramps Up Threat to Test Hydrogen Bomb over Pacific," *The Guardian*, October 25, 2017.

"North Korea's Nuclear Programme: How Advanced Is It?" BBC, last updated August 10, 2017. As of February 16, 2021: https://www.bbc.com/news/world-asia-pacific-11813699

"No Sign North Korea Reprocessed Plutonium in Past Year, Still Enriching Uranium, IAEA Says," Reuters, September 2, 2020.

Nuclear Threat Initiative, "Module 4: Case Study—North Korea's Scud Story," webpage, undated. As of February 16, 2021: https://tutorials.nti.org/delivery-system/case-study-north-koreas-scud-story/

———, CNS North Korea Missile Test Database, October 16, 2020. As of February 25, 2021: https://www.nti.org/analysis/articles/cns-north-korea-missile-test-database/

Nye, Joseph S., Jr., "North Korea's Powerful Weakness," *Project Syndicate*, July 11, 2013.

Oberdorfer, Don, *The Two Koreas: A Contemporary History*, New York: Basic Books, 1997.

Pabian, Frank V., Joseph S. Bermudez, Jr., and Jack Liu, "North Korea's Punggye-ri Nuclear Test Site: Satellite Imagery Shows Post-Test Effects and New Activity in Alternate Tunnel Portal Areas," 38 North, September 12, 2017. As of February 18, 2021: https://www.38north.org/2017/09/punggye091217/

Page, Jeremy, "China Prepares for a Crisis Along North Korea Border," *Wall Street Journal*, July 24, 2017.

Panda, Ankit, "US Intelligence: North Korea May Already Be Annually Accruing Enough Fissile Material for 12 Nuclear Weapons," *The Diplomat*, August 9, 2017.

———, *Kim Jong Un and the Bomb: Survival and Deterrence in North Korea*, New York: Oxford University Press, 2020.

"Park Pledges Strong Defense to Render N. Korean Nukes Useless," *Korea Herald*, October 1, 2013.

Park Won Gon, *Strategic Implications of the USFK Relocation to Pyeongtaek*, Seoul, South Korea: Korea Institute for Defense Analyses, No. 164, October 20, 2017. As of February 18, 2021: https://www.kida.re.kr/frt/board/frtPcrmBoardDetail.do?sidx=366&idx=2518&depth=3&search Condition=&searchKeyword=&pageIndex=7&lang=kr

pbr@yna.co.kr, "N. Korea Threatens Ultra-Harsh Action on U.S. Soil over Hacking Allegation," Yonhap News Agency, December 21, 2014.

Pearson, James, "North Korea Nuclear Blast Shows 'Uncanny Resemblance' to Last Test—Analyst," Reuters, January 8, 2016.

Perlangeli, Sara, "Flagging Down North Korea on the High Seas," Royal United Services Institute, March 29, 2018. As of February 18, 2021: https://rusi.org/commentary/flagging-down-north-korea-high-seas

Photo of Kim Jong-Un observing a missile test launch, distributed by Yonhap News Agency, 2016. As of February 24, 2021: http://img.yonhapnews.co.kr/etc/inner/EN/2016/07/20/AEN20160720001252315_04_i.jpg

Posto, Theodore A., "North Korean Ballistic Missiles and US Missile Defense," *Physics & Society*, Vol. 47, No. 2, April 2018, pp. 4–27.

Pritchard, Charles L., "A Guarantee to Bring Kim into Line," Brookings Institution, October 10, 2003. As of February 17, 2021: https://www.brookings.edu/opinions/a-guarantee-to-bring-kim-into-line/

"Project 2319 Tianbo [Sky Wave]: Over-the-Horizon Backscatter Radar [OTH-B]," GlobalSecurity.org, undated. As of August 18, 2020: http://www.globalsecurity.org/wmd/world/china/oth-b.htm

Ramani, Samuel, "The Long History of the Pakistan–North Korea Nexus," *The Diplomat*, August 30, 2016.

"Residents of N. Korea's Embattled Cities Face Starvation amid Continuing Coronavirus Blockade," *Rimjin-gang*, December 16, 2020. As of February 17, 2021: http://www.asiapress.org/rimjin-gang/2020/12/society-economy/starvation/

Ridgell, Clynt, "North Korea Threatened Guam Numerous Times in the Past," Pacific News Center, August 9, 2017.

Roh Suk-jo, "N.Korea 'Could Have 30–40 Nukes Next Year,'" *Chosun Ilbo*, September 17, 2019. As of February 22, 2021: http://english.chosun.com/site/data/html_dir/2019/09/17/2019091701515.html

Roy, Edward, "Bush Administration Unmoved by North Korea's Nuclear Statements," ABC, June 10, 2003.

Samuels, David, "How Osama Bin Laden Outsmarted the U.S. and Got What He Wanted," *Tablet*, January 22, 2014.

Sanger, David E., and Choe Sang-Hun, "Two Years After Trump-Kim Meeting, Little to Show for Personal Diplomacy," *New York Times*, June 12, 2020.

Sayle, Timothy Andrews, "A Nuclear Education: The Origins of NATO's Nuclear Planning Group," *Journal of Strategic Studies*, Vol. 43, No. 6–7, 2020, pp. 920–956.

"Senior N. Korean Official Says Its Nuke Program Targets No Country But U.S.," Yonhap News Agency, November 26, 2017.

Ser Myo-ja, "Park Tells Military to Strike Back If Attacked," *JoongAng Daily*, April 1, 2013.

Shalal, Andrea, David Brunnstrom, and Jonathan Landay, "North Korea Nuclear Test Did Not Increase Technical Capability: U.S.," Reuters, January 19, 2016.

Sharp, Andy, "North Korea Threatens to Use Nuclear Weapon to 'Sink' Japan," NDTV, last updated September 14, 2017. As of February 17, 2021:
https://www.ndtv.com/world-news/
north-korea-threatens-to-use-nuclear-weapon-to-sink-japan-1750144

Shim Kyu-seok, "North Korea Scoffs at Another Summit with Trump," *JoongAng Daily*, July 5, 2020. As of February 19, 2021:
https://koreajoongangdaily.joins.com/2020/07/05/national/northKorea/
north-korea-choe-sonhui-refusal/20200705171100439.html

Shin Hyon-hee, "N.K. Says Missile Test Aimed at Ports, Airfields in the South," *Korea Herald*, July 20, 2016. As of February 15, 2021:
http://www.koreaherald.com/view.php?ud=20160720000876

Smith, Alexander, "North Korea Launched No Missiles in 2018. But That Isn't Necessarily Due to Trump," NBC News, last updated December 31, 2018.

Smith, Josh, "'Treasured Sword': North Korea Seen as Reliant as Ever on Nuclear Arsenal as Talks Stall," Reuters, November 13, 2018.

———, "North Korea Nuclear Reactor Site Threatened by Recent Flooding, U.S. Think-Tank Says," Reuters, August 12, 2020.

Smith, Shane, *North Korea's Evolving Nuclear Strategy*, Washington, D.C.: US-Korea Institute at SAIS, August 2015a. As of February 19, 2021:
https://www.38north.org/wp-content/uploads/2015/09/
NKNF_Evolving-Nuclear-Strategy_Smith.pdf

———, *Implications for US Extended Deterrence and Assurance in East Asia*, Washington, D.C.: US-Korea Institute at SAIS, November 2015b. As of February 19, 2021:
https://www.38north.org/wp-content/uploads/2015/11/
NKNF-Smith-Extended-Deterrence-Assurance.pdf

———, "Renewing US Extended Deterrence Commitments Against North Korea," 38 North, May 13, 2020. As of February 19, 2021:
https://www.38north.org/2020/05/ssmith051320/

Stockholm International Peace Research Institute, *SIPRI Yearbook 2019: Armaments, Disarmament and International Security*, Oxford, United Kingdom: Oxford University Press, 2019.

Stokes, Mark A., *China's Nuclear Warhead Storage and Handling System*, Arlington, Va.: Project 2049 Institute, March 12, 2010. As of February 18, 2021:
https://project2049.net/2010/03/12/chinas-nuclear-warhead-storage-and-handling-system/

Tertrais, Bruno, "Destruction Assurée: The Origins and Development of French Nuclear Strategy, 1945-81," in Henry D. Sokolski, ed., *Getting MAD: Nuclear Mutual Assured Destruction, Its Origins and Practice*, Strategic Studies Institute, U.S. Army War College, 2004, pp. 51–122. As of February 17, 2021:
https://ssi.armywarcollege.edu/
getting-mad-nuclear-mutual-assured-destruction-its-origins-and-practice/

Thae Yong-Ho, member of the National Assembly of the Republic of Korea, "The Korean Peninsula Issues and US National Security," virtual address to Institute for Corean-American Studies, ICAS Winter Symposium, December 17, 2020.

UN—*See* United Nations.

United Nations Security Council, *Final Report of the Panel of Experts Submitted Pursuant to Resolution 2464*, New York, S/2020/151, March 2, 2020. As of February 19, 2021: https://www.un.org/securitycouncil/sanctions/1718/panel_experts/reports

U.S. Department of Defense, *Deterrence Operations: Joint Operating Concept*, Version 2.0, Washington, D.C., December 2006. As of February 18, 2021: https://www.jcs.mil/Portals/36/Documents/Doctrine/concepts/ joc_deterrence.pdf?ver=2017-12-28-162015-337

———, *Summary of the 2018 National Defense Strategy of the United States of America: Sharpening the American Military's Competitive Edge*, Washington, D.C., 2018a. As of February 18, 2021: https://dod.defense.gov/Portals/1/Documents/pubs/2018-National-Defense-Strategy-Summary.pdf

———, *Nuclear Posture Review*, Washington, D.C., February 2018b. As of February 18, 2021: https://media.defense.gov/2018/Feb/02/2001872886/-1/-1/1/ 2018-Nuclear-Posture-Review-Final-Report.pdf

U.S. Nuclear Regulatory Commission, "Uranium Enrichment," webpage, last updated December 2, 2020. As of February 17, 2021: https://www.nrc.gov/materials/fuel-cycle-fac/ur-enrichment.html

Vartabedian, Ralph, "North Korea Has Made a Nuclear Weapon Small Enough to Fit on a Missile. How Worried Should the World Be?" *Los Angeles Times*, August 9, 2017.

Vick, Charles, "Nodong," Federation of American Scientists, October 20, 2016. As of February 17, 2021: https://fas.org/nuke/guide/dprk/missile/nd-1.htm

Volodzko, David Josef, "China Wins Its War Against South Korea's US THAAD Missile Shield —Without Firing a Shot," *South China Morning Post*, November 18, 2017.

———, "North Korea Dangerous But Not Unpredictable, Says US Intelligence Official," NK News, January 22, 2021.

Waltz, Kenneth, *The Spread of Nuclear Weapons: More May Better*, London, United Kingdom: International Institute for Strategic Studies, *Adelphi Papers*, No. 171, 1981.

Wellerstein, Alex, NUKEMAP 2.7, tool, last updated 2020. As of February 23, 2021: https://nuclearsecrecy.com/nukemap/

Wertz, Daniel, *North Korea's Ballistic Missile Program*, Washington, D.C.: National Committee on North Korea, December 2017. As of February 17, 2021: https://www.ncnk.org/resources/briefing-papers/all-briefing-papers/ north-koreas-ballistic-missile-program

Whang, Jooho, *Research on Nuclear Threat Crisis Management Countermeasures in Neighboring Countries in Terms of Nuclear Nonproliferation and Nuclear Security*, Seongnam, South Korea: Korea Foundation of Nuclear Safety, July 10, 2019. As of February 25, 2021: https://nsrm.kofons.or.kr/uss/guide/report/formReport.do#AC=/uss/guide/report/ retrieveBoardList.do?bbsId=BBSMSTR_000000000005&VA= content_body&menuNo=9000006000

Wolf, Jim, "N.Korea Closer to Nuclear-Tipped Missile: U.S. Expert," Reuters, December 27, 2011.

About the Authors

Bruce W. Bennett is an adjunct international and defense researcher at the RAND Corporation. His primary research topics include strategy, force planning, and counterproliferation, and his research has addressed such issues as future ROK military force requirements, understanding and shaping the ongoing Korean nuclear weapon crisis, Korean unification, and deterrence of nuclear threats. Bennett holds a Ph.D. in policy analysis.

Kang Choi is the vice president for research and a principal fellow at the Asan Institute for Policy Studies. He writes extensively on the ROK-U.S. alliance, North Korean military affairs, inter-Korean relations, crisis management, and multilateral security cooperation. Choi holds a Ph.D. in political science.

Myong-Hyun Go is a senior research fellow at the Asan Institute for Policy Studies. His research applies quantitative perspectives to traditional and nontraditional security issues, with a special focus on North Korea's economy, sanctions, and the regime's long-term viability. Go is widely cited by the international media on North Korea and Northeast Asian security. He holds a Ph.D. in policy analysis.

Bruce E. Bechtol, Jr., is a professor of political science at Angelo State University. His primary research topics include North Korean military capabilities, North Korean military strategy and tactics, sanctions, and counterproliferation. His research has addressed North Korea's power and politics, abilities to attack the ROK and disrupt the region, and proliferation (including WMD) all over the world. Bechtol holds a Ph.D. in national security studies.

Jiyoung Park is a senior fellow at the Asan Institute for Policy Studies. Her main research areas are science, technology, and security policy. Her current interests include policy and management issues on nuclear technology, security challenges of emerging technology, and evidence-based science and technology policy. Park holds a Ph.D. in nuclear engineering and radiological sciences.

Bruce Klingner is a senior research fellow at the Heritage Foundation, where he specializes in Korean and Japanese affairs. He served 20 years in the Central Intelligence Agency and the Defense Intelligence Agency, where he was responsible for analysis of political and military issues for senior U.S. policymakers. Klingner holds master's degrees in national security strategy and strategic intelligence.

Du-Hyeogn Cha is a principal fellow of the Asan Institute for Policy Studies. He is a North Korea expert who has researched North Korean politics and military affairs, the U.S.-ROK alliance, and national crisis management. He also served as a research fellow at the Korea Institute for Defense Analyses for more than 20 years. Cha holds a Ph.D. in international relations.